SECRET FOLK-LORE
RUSSIAN STORIES

Illustrations de J. WELY
encadrements de G. DOLA

Stories *from the* Folk-lore
of
Russia

Erotic Tales of the Cossacks

« *Rouskiya Zavetnuiya Skazki* » done into English by the Translator of « The Book of Exposition in the Science of Coition. » « The Old Man Young Again »; and other charming works *ejusdem farinæ.*

Fredonia Books
Amsterdam, The Netherlands

Stories From the Folklore of Russia:
Erotic Tales of the Cossacks

ISBN: 1-4101-0503-2

Reprinted from the 1897 edition

Fredonia Books
Amsterdam, The Netherlands
http://www.fredoniabooks.com

In order to make original editions of historical works available to scholars at an economical price, this facsimile of the original edition of 1897 is reproduced from the best available copy and has been digitally enhanced to improve legibility, but the text remains unaltered to retain historical authenticity.

CONTENTS

TRANSLATOR'S   FOREWORD

To the Frivolous who, deceived by appearances, are ready to cry out : " What a shocking book! " " Why ever was it printed? " and who straightway would place this collection under the patronage of Cyprys the Lascivious and of her pretty son, Eros, we may say at once that we have chosen for Saint, the grave and chaste Athenais, the austere goddess of Wisdom and Science. We owe this declaration as much to ourselves as to our readers, for fear of the Profane and the Ungodly, or worse still, that more terrible foe — smug-faced " Mother Grundy. "

> " The Godly dame who fleshly failings damns
> Scolds with her maid, or with her Chaplain crams ;
> Would you enjoy soft nights and solid dinners
> Faith, gallants, board with saints and bed with sinners (1)."

At the outset of our observations, we think it fit to combat a popular misconception regarding the word " *folk-lore.* " Many persons, otherwise well-informed,

(1) Alexander Pope.

wrongly think that folk-lore relates to stories about
" Jack-and-the-Bean-stalk, " " Cinderella and the Glass
Slipper, " and other pretty legends of the kind told to
keep good little girls and boys from howling at bed-
time.

The present tales are nothing of the sort. Full of
homely jest and Rabelaisian humour, they deal with
incidents that a child — not yet stricken with the *fin de
siecle* disease, which so worries Max Nordau (1) —
would find it impossible to understand. But their star-
tling plainness of speech is not of the obscene kind that
deliberately chooses a word *because* it is coarse. If the
actors in these realistic scenes " call a spade a spade, "
it is because they have not learnt to veneer over, with
hypocritical phrase, actions that to them are as innocent as eating and drinking.

All those who busy themselves with popular and
traditional literature, — or to employ the excellent and
concise expression, folk-lore now almost universally
adopted, — have had occasion to meet on their way,
under the multifarious forms which they affect, tales,
songs, sayings and proverbs which are worthy of being
preserved and published. Some of these are remarkable
from a purely literary point of view, for their sparkling
liveliness and wit, others, more rarely it is true, by
their captivating style and graceful coquetry, and
others still because they offer an element of study and
comparison to folk-lorists. But the crudity and immorality of the subject, and the coarseness of the
expression employed have repelled collectors, who, in

(1) See " DEGENERATION " London (Heineman), 1895. Also his
" CONVENTIONAL LIES OF OUR CIVILIZATION. "

general, have allowed the materials they had brought together to fall again into oblivion.

Nevertheless, a great number of these, thanks mainly to the literary Workers of the Middle Ages, and of the Renaissance, particularly in Italy and France, — less prudish or less hypocritical than those of today — have been handed down to us in the form of Ancient Lays, Rhymed Legends, Satirical Dramas, Farces, and Tales, more or less disguised and travestied, and shorn of their original coarse cynicism. It is true that the world, generally, knows nothing about them, sleeping as they do on the manuscript shelves of public or private libraries. Moreover the *savants* who brought the most celebrated of these collections of legends together, have hitherto not dared to interrupt their dusty slumbers and to insert them in their rightful place among other documents. There is here a curious mine to work, and many a treasure to bring to light for which, some day perhaps, we may find the opportunity. Some of them, and not the least obscene, have had the good fortune to appear in some famous collections as, for instance " le Lai des quatre souhaits Saint-Martin " (*Barbazan-Méon collection*, vol. IV). We also possess a literary version of the tale of the " Ridiculous Wishes, " as curious as it is gross, but of which the gaiety and wit excuse the rank obscenity. Happily also, more than one tale of obscene form has been easily made, by means of a few slight and unimportant changes, to take on such a decent aspect as to be capable of being related for the amusement of children, or of circulating in polite and elegant society. To give but one example, " Les Souhaits ridicules. " Perrault had merely in this tale to suspend the " yard of sausage " to the nose of the peasant's wife in order to render one of the very numerous versions of this funny story fit to take place in a collection destined for children.

Similarly, in the tales belonging to the same family as those of which the Tree Nose of Grimm is the type, it is not *in the popular version,* the *nose* but another organ which lengthens out, stretching away for many a league and following which its owner may be found by tracing it along through by paths and bushes.

When such simple substitutions could be made, without injuring the narrative, it was all right from every point of view. But it is not always so. There certainly exists — our collection will prove it — some popular versions whose curious obscenity under more than one heading is such, that there is no pen, however skillful or experienced that could reproduce them without perverting their meaning; owing to which they have lost their primitive intention to the great detriment of folk-lore science. That the obscene version of a tale should be left unnoticed is the more to be regretted because it often constitutes the primitive form which, with other readings and interpolations, has given rise to better known and more decent narratives, but which from the particular standpoint of the folklorist have less interest. For instance, it is not necessary to be a specialist to see in the two forms of the obscene feature that is met with in Rabelais's and in La Fontaine's story of *Le Diable de Papefiguiere* and in several of the following Cossack stories, that it was the popular form which preceded the literary. And yet it is certain that the coarse and ignorant *moujiks* who recount these stories never heard either of Rabelais or of La Fontaine; it was from popular tradition that they culled them. Rabelais and after him the fabulist, La Fontaine, threw it again into library form. — Besides the immorality of a work does not consist in the crudity of the words, and the coarseness of the expression, but the object had in view by the writer. Take any of the great classics, so dear to us; — the old Hebrew books; the rollicking comedies of the Elizabethan playwrights; the naive stories of Queen Margaret's women; the audaciously free tales of Boccaccio; and half-a-score more; and it will be found that any attempt to castrate or gloze over their scurrilousness would be to destroy that healthy, full-blooded vitality in them which for us makes them so intensely human. The most perverse novels of the XVIII century are often written in a chastened style where the flowers of language distil deadly poison. — No matter to what nation or to what century he may belong, a writer who seeks to kindle evil passions in the minds of his readers, even though he write in the most correct and irreproachable style, must be considered immoral.

The ex-priest, Liseux, may be aptly cited here. Editor of a series of pornographic works, he was as fair minded as learned, and his words have therefore double weight. In the short " *avertissement* " to his edition in French of these skazki, he says:

"Dans notre conviction, toutefois, si ces contes offensent quelque chose de respectable, c'est plutot le gout que les moeurs. Leur obscénité meme leur confere une

sorte d'innocuité morale; ils sont trop cyniques pour
etre voluptueux. De meme que le spectacle de l'ivresse
enseigne la sobriété, rien n'est plus propre a refroidir
l'ardeur des sens que l'étalage brutal des choses de
l'amour. Certes, nous ne voudrions pas conseiller cette
lecture a la virginité ignorante, mais peut-etre la re-
commanderions-nous moins encore a la caducité en
quete d'excitations érotiques. Les vieillards qui deman-
dent a une lecture spéciale le *stimulus veneris,* ne
trouveraient pas ici ce qu'ils cherchent."

As for the employment of obscene words, their immorality is altogether contingent, being a question
which varies with the age and the country. No better
example can be cited than certain well-known passages
in the Bible, or in the very grave and most pious
dissertations of the Scholiasts on subjects which are
themselves most scabrous.

We consider then that we are adding yet another
stone to the lordly building of Human Knowledge in
publishing this collection, whose contents, however
gross, scatalogical, and obscene they may appear, yet
afford to the thinker and philosopher a real insight into
popular traditions and customs, and constitute human
documents more precious than all theorisings. There is
deep truth, as well as fine writing, in the words Goethe
so ably puts into Mephistoles's mouth:

Grey, my dearest friend, is all thy theory,
And green the golden tree of life.

We may add that these tales have a two-fold value
to the folk-lorist and observer, for whilst they stimu-
late his zeal to solve some of the questions which they

raise, they also aid him with clues to some of the problems which have long puzzled him. Russia is, physically and intellectually, a barrier between Europe and Asia. On the one side Western civilization surges against it; on the other side it is laved by Eastern influences, rich in sensuous imaginings and legends that were old already when Europe was inhabited by a horde of savages, and neither of these mighty oceans has *apparently* had any effect on the twinship of ignorance and indifference that distinguishes the Russian peasant and his barbarous brother Cossack.

Apparently, we say advisedly, for curiously under more headings than one, our *Secret Russian Stories* are strikingly remarkable for their resemblance to certain tales believed to be peculiar to given peoples. Manifold are the traces of Eastern and Western folklore, which would seem to form the connecting link between the prolific inventions of the one and profound superstition of the other. Below the ice-bound rocks of Russia may, perhaps in a way, flow the secret current that connects the two oceans.

Without doubt we shall more than once have to silence our scruples, to overcome our repugnance. But we think that Science like fire, purifies all. — Like the chemist who weighs, analyses and synthetizes the least tempting substances, without being affected by their aspect or their odour; like the doctor who describes the most intimate details and studies the most mysterious functions of the organs of generation, solely for science's sake, so also shall we if need be, touch with chaste hand and mind unsullied, subjects the most scurrilous, details of Sadisian obscenity or immorality the most revolting. However, it is not in vain that the old English blood courses through our veins, and besides as Rabelais says: *Rire est le propre de l'homme,* we shall not therefore when the place calls it forth seek to stifle back the honest, frank laugh, free from low idea and coarse thought, which the reading of Beaumont and Fletcher or the Novels of Sterne, Smollett and Fielding always bring to lips that speak the Anglo-Saxon tongue, or the sly smile evoked by the slightly more refined writings of the Queen Anne period.

Our publication is exclusively destined for folk-lorists, and our object to avoid those who in the dung of Ennius see only the filthy heap while overlooking the glittering pearls his genius has flung there.

The series now commencing with the stories of South Russia will, we trust, include later the Tales and folk-lore productions of all nations.

By means of these recitals we may see how the *jinn* became converted into the witch; — the brother of the Fairy *Paribanou* might have come straight from *Gotenheim*; — and the subtle analysis of the folk-lorist may detect again some of the same metal in Solomon's ring and Thor's hammer. Even with the very limited knowledge possessed by the present writer he can discover in many of these tales analogies to some of the apologues of the *Pancha-Tantra of Pilpay*; No. XXVII is but another version of " The old man who was going to mind the house, " — as related by Grimm, whilst, singular to say, No. I calls to mind the adventures of Brer Rabbit and Brer Fox.

The Cossack tales in this volume are translated from a collection in the Little Russian dialect, published in

a limited edition. The original, from which our version
is translated, exists in the *Bibliotheque Nationale,*
Paris, and consists of a small unbound in-8° book of
about 200 pages. No author's name figures on the title
page and the only indication of its origin consists of
the following rather enigmatic superscription :

"BALAAM
PRINTED ON THE PRESSES OF THE MONASTIC
BROTHERHOOD
IN THE YEAR OF THE DEVILRY OF GLOOM. "

Our version is the first that has yet appeared in the
English language. A French text was issued by our old
friend, Isidore Liseux, and edited with his customary
care, but without illustrations or annotations, moreover
it was prepared solely for French bibliophiles and
book-amateurs. W. R. Ralston, M.A. (1), makes a
guarded allusion to our collection in the following
words: *There is one other recent collection of Skazkas
(2), that published last year at Geneva under the title
of "Russkiya Zavetnuiya Skazki." But upon its
contents I have not found it necessary to draw.* It is to
be regretted that the fear of Mother Grundy gagged
the mouth of this talented scholar. Occupying a post at
the British Museum, had he been bold enough to
embody his knowledge of these stories in his able work
on the folk-tales of Russia, he would have undoubtedly
paid for his ill-timed temerity with his situation, although he would have risen in the esteem of all real

(1) " Russian Folk-tales, " London (Trübner), 1873, Preface xi.
(2) *i.e.,* Folk-tales, SKAZKAS is a plural formed on an English model—
the real Russian plural of the word is, of course, SKAZKI.

scholars. Less able by far, without the wonderful knowledge, nor having the great opportunities of research that he commanded, we have ventured to issue our version, but disclaim all pretentions to completeness. Let it be regarded as a pioneer work, undertaken in the face of fire when those stronger intellectually hung back. Our object is not " Pornography for the sake of Pornography, " but " Pornography for the sake of Science. " When the vagaries, obscenities, and wayward fancies of Human Nature are collected, ticketed and docketed *as such,* they will lose their perniciousness, and be relegated to what a clever French *litérateur* terms *le Musée d'Anatomie Erotique* (1) Men are beginning to envisage this question from the right standpoint, and already a larger freedom (2) of expression in the discussion of the sexual relations of men and women is, in spite of all the spleen and resistance of the Philistines, demanded and allowed.

We have reproduced the text just as it is, notwithstanding its unheard of coarseness of language and, what is worse, of ideas; a coarseness which is a testimony, alas, too convincing, to customs curious for more reasons than one. These stories furnish many points of comparison with other well-known tales, more especially with the new Italian and French *Contes joyeux* of the Renaissance, for which they may stand

(1) OCTAVE UZANNE, in " NOS AMIS LES LIVRES, " p. 62 Paris (QUANTIN), 1896.

(2) For instance Havelock Ellis's book " SEXUAL INVERSION; STUDIES IN THE PSYCHOLOGY OF SEX" (1897) Krafft-Ebing's "PSYCHOPATHIA SEXUALIS "; and last, but by no means least, Farmer Henley's "SLANG AND ITS ANALOGUES" (6 vol.) 1896-97, probably the most complete lexicon of Heterodox Speech that has ever appeared. About 18 columns of synonymous words are given to express that spot in lovely Woman nestling midway between the thighs and navel ! !

as the popular version. The specimens of satirical
popular stories are far less frequent than the marvel-
ous or mythical. This is the characteristic of the
present work. A rather piquant detail, as intimated
above, is that these tales were gathered by an orthodox
monk, for the greater glory of science, and printed by
the monastic printing press, in order to evade the
Russian censure. They in general contain very bitter
satires against the *popes,* as the Russian priests are
called, which gives them a feature of resemblance with
the French writers of ancient versified tales, who were
always pleased to bring monks and nuns forward upon
the scene in the least edifying positions.

It may to some people seem astonishing that Russian *moujiks* could print such satires against their
spiritual *confréres,* the priests. To this we reply that
there exists in Russia a very pronounced antagonism
between the lower classes and the regular clergy — i.e.
— the *popes* and the *moujiks* — who, with the hatred
of their kind, show each other no mercy.

The same thing has been seen in France and in
Italy. Rabelais, the jovial vicar of Meudon, did not
hesitate to put into the mouth of monks and nuns the
most risky expressions, for which, he would have certainly answered with his life, but for the protection of
Francis the First. Firenzuola, the well-known Benedic-
tine friar, was another incorrigible *farceur,* who threw
into the form of lively *novelettes* his outspoken appre-
ciations of the vices of the Italian clergy.

A similar, although perhaps not exactly parallel
case, may be found in the ridicule heaped at the
Restoration on the English Puritans, who were ex-

posed, as Macaulay points out, to the utmost licentiousness of the Press and the Stage, when the Press and the Stage were the most licentious, and whose sour aspect, nasal twang, stiff posture, long graces, Hebrew names, Scriptural phrases, and other foibles were abandoned to the Satirists and Dramatists, and became fair game for the Churchmen and the laughers in general.

If evidence be required as to the kinship of Races, we find it in this volume. Nothing is recondite or far-fetched. These old Russian stories turn upon pivots which, as Ralston well says, are *familiar to all the world, and have for their themes such common-place topics as the incorrigible folly of man, the inflexible obstinacy of woman.* They form a volume of facetiae which have figured as the stock-in-trade of rustic Falstaffs and Sancho Panzas whether among the vineyards of France or Germany, or on the hills of Greece, or beside the Norway fiords, or along the coasts of Brittany or the Scottish Highlands—facetiae which, for centuries, have set grey-beards wagging in Cairo or Ispahan, or excited the sensuous brains of the warm-blooded sons and daughters of dusky Burmah and Bengal.

Let us now hear what the patient searcher has to say, who took down these stories as they fell, from the lips of *moujiks* and of soldiers, and by courageously putting the interests of Science above vulgar prejudice, has so well earned the thanks of all earnest students.

The issuing of these secret tales, in the form and order in which we present them to Scholars and Amateurs, constitutes a fact almost unique in its kind. It

may happen, precisely for that very reason, that this
book will provoke reproaches and exclamations of all
kinds, not only against the daring editor, but also
against the nation which has given birth to such tales,
wherein popular fancy has, without the least restraint
of language, unfolded, in sparkling pictures, all the
force and richness of its humour. Putting aside all the
reproaches addressed personally to ourselves, we must
declare that any outcry uttered against the national
wit would be not only an injustice, but, indeed, evidence of that deep-seated ignorance which is, in most
cases, one of the most indelible features of querulous
prudery.

Our " Secret Tales " as we have already hinted,
stand forth as a venture unique in its kind, because
there does not exist, to our knowledge, another edition
in which the genuine popular language flashed out in
such abundance, overflowing with all the brilliant and
ingenious traits of the man of the people.

The literature of other nations abounds in secret
stories of the same nature and many of them have long
since seen the light, not perhaps in the form of tales,
but in that of Songs, Dialogues, Novelettes, Farces,
Satirical Dramas, Moralities, and Proverbs. Other nations possess an enormous number of productions in
which popular wit, equally free from all restraint of
expression and figure, enlivens with humour, smites
with satire, or boldly holds up to laughter, various
phases of life.

Who indeed can for a moment doubt that the jocund
stories of Boccaccio were drawn from popular life; that
the innumerable French novelettes and facetiae ema-

nated from the same source; that the satirical efforts of
the Spaniards; the *spottlieder* (1) and the
Schmaehschriften (2) of the Germans; that the mass of
pasquinades, of divers stray sayings in all languages,
which appear in connection with all possible incidents
of public and private life, sprang originally from the
people?

In Russian literature, it is true, there still exists a
crowd of popular expressions which have not yet been
printed and *were not destined to be printed.* In the
literature of other nations, such barriers to the language of the people have long ceased to exist. Without
going back to classical antiquity, we may take the
Ragionamenti of Pietro Aretino, the *Capitoli* of Franc
Berni; of Giov. della Casa of Molza; the *Rettorica
delle Putanne* of Pallavicini; the *Alcibiade Fanciullo
a scola*; to say nothing of the intellectual offspring of
many other Italian writers *the Elegantiae Latini Ser-
monis* of Meursius; the whole series, in French Literature, of the celebrated *joyeusetez, faceties et folastres
imaginations*; the famous *Recueil de pieces choisies
par les soins du Cosmopolite* — and we see without
doubt that all this mass of *Flugschriften* which as
Schade says: " then overflowed the land like a deluge
(3), " that it was not in that age deemed necessary to
hide the printed word beneath the veil of startled
prudery or under the fig-leaf of a writing chastened by
the censure. Is it necessary to call to mind the Maca-
ronic lucubrations which were so highly esteemed from

(1) Bantering songs.
(2) Scandalous pamphlets.
(3) " Damals wie ein Fluth übers Land fuhren. "

the time of Lorenzo de' Medici the Magnificent, to that
of the Medicis of a more recent period? It would,
finally, be sheer waste of time to dwell on the fact that
such writings are solely reserved for the delectation of
bibliophiles, and that there are entire series of the
same kind, the subjects of which are amply described
in special bibliographies, such as the *Bibliotheca Ar-
cana*. These works are known to the book-world under
the titles of *Singularités, Curiosa, Ouvrages sur
l'Amour, Sur la Galanterie, Facetiae,* and so forth. And,
far more important, the noble collection of Pisanus
Fraxi, brought out under the title of *Index Librorum
Prohibitorum, Absconditorum* and *Tacendorum,* which
are the only books dealing, in an adequate manner,
specially with English erotic works.

The reproach of gross cynicism, addressed to the
Russian nation, is equivalent to the same reproach
made to all other nations or, in other words, amounts
to no reproach at all, as being common to all.

For the erotic contents of the " Secret Russian Tales "
proves nothing either for or against the morality of
the Russian people. Prominence is simply given to one
side of popular life, which more than any other excites
humour, satire and irony. These stories are delivered
in a form devoid of art, just as they rolled out from the
lips of the common folk, and are written down in the
coarse-mouthed tale-tellers *ipsissima verba.* It is that
which gives them their distinctive character.

Pisanus Fraxi well says: *The immoral lubricity
which emanates from the perverted brain of a man of
culture, and has for its object the excitement of the
passions, is entirely absent,* but the rough, gross fun, so

dear to the uneducated, where each object is called by
its common name, each act or incident told in a plain
unvarnished manner, abounds. They reveal to us in an
interesting and unequivocal way, the feelings, aspira-
tions, modes of thought, manner of living of the people
who tell them, and *are possibly one of the most
valuable contributions to the study of folk-lore which
has yet appeared.* "

This book is not intended for " Tom, Dick or Harry "
to sniggle and smirk over, but for the Thinker, and
Scholar, and in general those who see no shamefulness
in the naturalness of Nature. Words are employed, it is
true, which shock the modest sensibilities of Western
ears; but such crudities, we repeat, are not used ob-
scenely. The teller of these tales is unacquainted with
circumlocutions, and perhaps would not use them if he
were. Were he more civilized he might be nicer in his
speech, but would inevitably acquire worse vices. Perhaps, when he learns " to speak by the card, his toe
may come so near to the heel of the courtier as to gall
his kibe. " It seems to the translator that to omit these
terms would be to detract from the value of the book.

This bluntness of speech in the Arabs struck Sir R.-F.
Burton as a praiseworthy quality, yet the Arab has
at his command a copious and poetical tongue, which
affords him a host of synonyms wherewith to gloss over
objectionable words, and the Russian peasant has next
to no literature, and is not — though perhaps wrongly
— credited with much imagination. For Fletcher,
Rochester, or Sterne, to employ the words which occur
so often in these tales is an offence against good taste;
but with the Slav ground-tiller it is different, for he has

no equivalents ready, and is not hampered by the same considerations as to taste.

In these tales, nothing has been changed or embellished, and nothing added. We merely insist upon the striking fact, that in the different zones of the vast Russian empire the same story may crop up under various aspects. There are numerous different versions, and doubtless most of them pass from mouth to mouth without having been as yet caught up and put into writing by studious collectors. Those which we publish have been chosen out of a number of the most remarkable and characteristic.

We think that it is superfluous for us to explain the order in which these tales appear. We wish only to draw attention to the fact that those in which animals are made to play a part give the best possible evidence of all the cuteness and vigourous observation of the peasant. Far from cities, labouring in the open fields, in the forest or on the river, he has everywhere a profound sympathy with Nature, the Well-beloved; he notes with preciseness, and learns to enter into the smallest details of the great, simple life in the midst of which " he moves and lives and has his being. " The phases of this life seized on the quick, — dumb to the dweller in cities — but full of eloquence for him, stamp themselves vividly upon his imagination and, at once and without study, we have a tale ready to hand, full of life and bright humour. That portion of the stories which relates to those, whom the people designate as the *stallion race,* and of which for the present we have given but a small part, sheds a searching light upon the relations between the *moujik* and his spiritual pastors and indicates the true way of understanding the character of these latter.

These secret Russian stories, curious from many points of view beside, are specially remarkable it seems to us, for the following reason: to the serious scholar and the profound investigator of the Russian national character, they supply a vast field of comparison with the almost identical subjects of other tales found in writers belonging to nations quite aloof from the Slavonic race. By what road did the tales of Boccaccio, the French satires and farcical stories of the XVI century penetrate into the remotest corners of the great virgin North? How did the Western *novelette* find a new life in these Russian *récits;* what feature have they in common? where are, and whence proceed, the traces of the influence? of what nature are the doubts and the conclusions to be drawn from such an identity?

Leaving the solutions of such questions and of many others to *ex cathedra* savants, we trust that our readers will find a good word for the labours of the worthy gatherers of these tales. On our part, in editing this rare collection, with the object of snatching it "as a brand from (fanatical) burning " we shall remain, we presume to think, equally indifferent to praise or censure.

Therefore, without hypocritically assuming a strict scientific appearance, our volume goes forth, garbed in the homely dress of a free and rough English version, to present to the world that side of the Humour of the Russian peasantry, which until to-day had been enshrined in no print, and incarnated in no book, as a rare, and precious literary treasure for the student of

Human Nature who, in such stories, is able to recognise invaluable data elucidating certain puzzling points of psychology, which may, after all, be deemed worth knowing.

END OF THE FOREWORD

LIST OF RUSSIAN WORDS

WHICH CROP UP NOW AND AGAIN IN THE TEXT (1)

Altar. — A sanctuary and a place often witness to
seductions.

Barine. — A lord, a gentleman who clambers upon his
serf's daughters.

Barinia. — A lady, who seeks consolation sometimes in
the robustness of the domestics.

Batko. — Father (colloquial).

Batouchka. — Little father (often applied to priests).

Blines. — Small pancakes.

Desiatine. — A surface measure equal to 2½ acres and
9/10 of a rood.

Diadioushka. — Little uncle.

Doushenka. — Little soul (term of endearment).

Izba. — Dwelling-place of the Russian peasant.

Kasha. — Gruel.

Matouchka. — Little mother.

Moujik. — Peasant.

Popadia. — Wife of a priest; and, in these tales, a rare
lecherous bitch.

Pope. — A derogatory term for *Sviashchennik,* the
parish priest.

Popovna. — Priest's daughter; she takes strongly after
her parents for heat of blood.

Shchi. — Cabbage soup.

Tsigane. — Gypsy.

Vershok. — A measure, a trifle over an inch.

---

(1) We have been obliged to retain these words in the translation, because no real equivalents for them exists in English.
Other expressions that may occur are explained *in loco.*

SECRET STORIES

of RUSSIAN FOLK-LORE

* * *

I

The vixen and the hare.

Spring had come, and its influence had aroused the sexual passions of a hare, who, though not very brave, was a bit of a rascal. He wandered through the woods, and determined to pay a visit to a certain vixen. When he got to the fox's den, she was lying on the stove, and the cubs were all looking out of the window. When she saw the hare, she said, " Listen to me, my children. If that scoundrel comes here, say I am not at home. It must be the devil sends him here. I have long owed the villain a grudge; perhaps this time I shall catch him one way or another. " Thereupon the vixen hid herself. The hare came and knocked at the door. " Who is there? " asked

the cubs. " It is I, " said the visitor. " How do
you do, my dears? Is your mother at home? "
" No, she is not. " — " That's a pity, for I came
on purpose to ride her — and now she is not at
home, " said the hare; and with that he scuttled
off through the wood.

The vixen had heard all that passed. " Oh,
you son of a bitch, " she cried. " Wait a bit, you
impudent rascal, and I will make you pay dearly
for your impudence. "

She jumped off the stove, and hid herself behind
the door, expecting that the hare would come
again. Very soon he did come back. " Good day,
my dears; is your mother at home? " he asked
the cubs. " She is not. " " So much the worse, "
replied the hare, " I would have given her her
fill of pleasure. " With that the vixen popped out
and said, " Good day, my friend. " The hare
scuttled away as fast as he could, and ran till
he was out of breath, dropping his dirt with
fright on the road. The vixen pursued him.
" You shall not escape this time, you ugly
scoundrel, " she cried. She was close upon him.
The hare made a bound, and jumped between
two birch trees, which grew close together. The
vixen tried to do the same, but she was caught
between the two trees, and could not, do all she
would, go forwards or backwards, though she
used all her efforts to regain her liberty. The
rascally hare looked behind him, and seeing how

luck had favoured him, he went back and satisfied his pleasure on the vixen. " That is the way we do it, " he said. When he had well trussed her, he ran away as fast as he could.

Not far from there was a cinder pit, where a peasant had been making a fire. The hare ran and wallowed in the black dust, till he looked like a real monk. Then he went back to the road, and walked quietly along with his ears down. Very soon up came the vixen, who had at last got free, and was looking after the hare; when she saw him she took him for a monk. " Good day, holy father, " she said, " have you seen an ugly, squinting hare pass this way? "

" What hare? The one who gave you such a doing just now? " The vixen blushed with shame and returned home as fast as she could. " Oh, the rascal, " she said, " he has already told

the story in all the monasteries. " Cunning as the vixen was, the hare could give her points.

II

The sparrow and the mare.

In the cow-yard of a peasant's house was a whole flock of sparrows. One of them began to boast to the others. " The grey mare, " he said, " is in love with me. She often gives me sly glances. Would you like to see me truss her in the presence of all this honourable company? " " Yes, we should like to see that, " replied the others. The sparrow flew to the mare, and said, " Good day, my dear little mare. " " Good day, little songster. What is it you want? " " Look here! I want to ask you to let me . . . " " Very well, " replied the mare; " In our country when a young man keeps company with a girl, it is customary for him to give her presents, and he buys her nuts and gingerbread. But as for you, what could you give me? " " Only tell me what you want. " " Very well, go and bring me, grain by grain, a *tchetverik* of oats (1), and then you can have me."

(1) A *tchetverik* is nearly three quarters of a bushel.

The sparrow set to work, and with much hard work succeeded at last in collecting a whole *tchetverik* of oats. Then it went and fluttered before the mare. " Come along, my dear, the oats are here. " But when it said this, the sparrow did not feel any impatience. " All right, " said the mare, " it is no good putting off the business. I can't expect to remain chaste all my life, and the affection of a fellow like you is not to be despised. Bring the oats, and call your comrades together; I am not ashamed to let you do what you like. Sit on my tail, close to my arse, and wait till I lift up my tail. "

The mare began to eat the oats, the sparrow sat on the mare's tail, and the other sparrows waited to see what would happen: The mare ate and ate, then it lifted up its tail and the sparrow quickly got into its backside. The mare squeezed him with her tail, and hurt him terribly. However, when she had finished eating, she began to fart. The sparrow came out in a hurry, and went and bragged to its comrades. " That is the way we fellows do it! The mare could not stand it any longer; did you hear how she farted? "

III

The bear and the peasant woman.

A peasant woman was working in a field; a bear saw her, and said to himself. " Only think. I have never fought with a woman. I wonder whether they are stronger than men! I have over-thrown plenty of men, but I never had anything to do with a woman. " He came up to the peasant woman and said, " I want to fight you. " " But suppose you should happen to rend me, Michael Ivanovitch? " " Why in that case I would give you a hive full of honey. " " Very well. Let us fight. " The bear seized the woman in his paws, and threw her on the ground. She threw her legs in the air, opened them wide, and said to him, " See what you have done! How can I show myself at home now? What shall I say to my husband? " The bear looked, and saw a great split. It was evidently his handiwork! He did not know what to do. Just then a hare ran by. " Wait a moment, " cried the bear, " Stop, and then come here. " The hare obeyed. The bear took the woman by the lips of her vulva, pulled them together, and told the hare to hold them whilst he hurried off to the wood to get some strips of bark. He came back with such a big bundle that he could scarcely carry it. He threw the bark on the ground, but the woman was frightened, and let a fart, which made the hare jump five feet away. " Why look, Michael Ivanovitch, she is split all round. " " Yes, now she is cracked on both sides, " said the bear, and ran away as fast as possible.

IV

The wolf.

A peasant had a sow which brought forth a litter of twelve pigs. He shut her up in a sty, the walls of which were made of brushwood pegged together. The next day the peasant went to look at his pigs; he counted them, and found there was one missing. The following day he found another sucking pig had disappeared. Who took them? The old man passed the night in the sty and watched. Out of the wood came a wolf which came straight to the stable, turned its back to the door, put its tail through a hole, and began to rub it in the floor of the sty. Attracted by the noise, the little pigs left their mother and came to the door to sniff at the wolf's tail. Then the wolf turned around, put its snout in at the hole from which it had just taken its tail, grabbled one of the young pigs, and carried it off to the woods.

The next evening the peasant came back to the pig-house, and seated himself close to the door. When it was quite pitch dark, the wolf came again, and tried the same trick as before, but as soon as it had slipped its tail in at the door, the peasant seized it with both hands, and putting his feet against the door began to cry with all his might " Tu! Tu! Tu! " The wolf made desperate endeavors to get free, and struggled so hard that at last its tail came off. The animal ran away, but it lost so much blood that when it had gone twenty yards, it fell on the ground and died. The peasant flayed it, and sold the skin.

V

The peasant, the bear, the fox, and the gad-fly.

The peasant did not know what to do to escape from his enemies. All at once an idea came to him; he seized his wife in his arms, and threw her on the ground. " Be quiet, " said her husband, and without letting her go, he pulled off her gown and her shift; then he raised her legs in the air as high as he could. The bear saw that

the peasant was hurting a woman. " No, friend
fox, " he said " you and the gad-fly may say what
you like, but nothing in the world shall persuade
me to come near the peasant. " " Why not ? "
" Look for yourself, and see how he is ill treating that poor woman. " Then the fox looked,
and said; " You are right. I'm sure he is break-
ing her legs. " The gad-fly looked in his turn.
" It's not that at all, " he said at last. " He
is putting a straw up her arse. " They all agreed
that it would be dangerous to attack the man,
but the gad-fly was nearer the truth than the
others. The bear and the fox ran off into the
wood, and the peasant returned home safe and
sound.

VI

The cat and the vixen.

A peasant had driven out of his house a ruttish
cat, which had gone to live in the woods. In
this wood also lived a whorish vixen who was
always sporting with the wolves and the bears.
She met the cat, and they began to talk about
this and that. " Kotofei Ivanovitch, " said the
vixen, " you are a bachelor, and I am not
married; take me for your wife. " The cat
consented. They made a great feast, and after

that indulged in amorous sports. The cat mounted on the vixen, but tore her with his claws more than he caressed her. However he continued to cry out : " Again, again, again! " " What a curious being, " said the vixen. " he never has enough. "

VII

The louse and the flea.

A louse met a flea. " Where are you going ? "
" I am going to pass the night in a woman's slit. "
" And I am going into a woman's backside. "
They parted. The next day they met again.
" Well, how did you sleep ? " asked the louse.
" Oh, don't talk about it. I was so frightened. A
kind of bald head came to me and hunted me
about. I jumped here and there, but he continued
to pursue me. At last he spat on me and went
away. " " Well, gossip, there were two persons
knocking about outside the hole I was in. I hid
myself, and they continued to push about, but at
last they went away. "

VIII

The woodpecker.

A peasant woman caught a woodpecker, and
put it in a cage. When her husband came home,
she told him how she had caught the bird.
" Where is this woodpecker ? You have not let
it fly away, have you ? " asked he. " I put it in
a cage, " replied the woman. " Very good! I

will soon settle its business ! I am going to eat
it alive. " He opened the cage, but as he was
going to give the first bite, the woodpecker flew
into his mouth, ran through his body and put
its head out of his arse and began to cry, " I'm
alive! I'm alive! " Then it disappeared, but
showed itself again soon afterwards, and repeated the same phrase. It gave the peasant no
rest, and, finding himself much troubled, he
said to his wife, " Get a cudgel. I will go on
my hands and knees, and when the woodpecker
shows itself, give it a good crack on the head. "
He went down on all fours, and his wife took
a thick stake, brandished it, and brought it
down as soon as the woodpecker's head appeared, but instead of hitting the bird, she bruised
the peasant's backside. What was to be done?
The poor man could not get rid of the woodpecker, which continued to poke its head out of
his arse and cry, " I'm alive ! I'm alive ! "
" Take a very sharp scythe, " said the *moujik*
to his wife. " I will again go down on all fours,
and as soon as the woodpecker's head comes
out, cut it off. " The woman took the scythe,
and her husband went down on his hands and
knees. No sooner had the bird's head appeared,
than the woman tried to cut it off, but she han-
dled the weapon clumsily, and only wounded the
moujik's arse. Then the bird flew away, and
the peasant died from loss of blood.

IX

The vagina and the arse.

A dispute arose one day between the c..t and the arse, and God only knows what a fuss they made. The vagina said to the arse, " You had better hold your tongue, you scoundrel. You know that I receive a nice visitor every night, and all the time you make a horrible stench. " " Oh, miserable slit, " replied the arse. " When you are being futtered, the spit falls upon me, and I have to hold my tongue. " All this happened in the good old days before knives were invented, and a man cut his meat with his tool.

X

Wash the bottom.

Once upon a time there lived a man and his wife; one day when the woman served her husband with his dinner, he began to beat her, and cried, " Wash the bottom; wash the bottom. " She went and washed her backside, and scrubbed it with sand, and rubbed it with a towel till the blood came. But as soon as she came back to the table, her husband again began to beat her and to cry, " Wash the bottom ; wash the bottom ! " The woman went and complained to her aunt. " I don't know what is the matter, aunt, " she said, " but as soon as I lay the table, my husband beats me, and cries, " Wash

the bottom ; wash the bottom. Yet I do wash my backside well, and rub it till the blood comes. " — " What a fool you are ; it is not your bottom that he means, but the bottom of the cup. " When the woman washed the bottom of the cup, her husband ceased to beat her.

XI

Bad, not bad.

A dog sat on a millstone which floated on the water; his head hung down, his tail was between his legs, he whined and licked his paws. " Have you passed by the bishop's house? " Yes ; the horses are saddled, the men are mounted, they are blowing trumpets, but the devil knows what they are celebrating. They say the bishop is being married to a dun mare . . . Have you seen Rostoff's bear? Yes. What is it like? Grey. Is it a bear? Go, and f . . k yourself! Don't say stupid things; it is a wolf. — Will you hold your tongue; in our country the wolf skulks in the woods and shakes his ears. — It is a hare. M... (1).

XII

The fool.

A peasant had a son who was very stupid. The young man wanted to get married, and sleep with a woman, and began to worry his father. " Let me get married, papa. " — " Wait a bit, my

(1) Different versions of this not over choice nursery jingle are found in various districts. The last word is the *mot de Cambronne* (a French euphemism for *merde,* i.e., shit).

son, " said the father. " It is too soon for you to
get married yet: Your tool does not yet reach
to your arse; when it does, you shall be married. " Then the youth took his member, and
pulled it as hard as he could, and then looked,
and saw that his father had told the truth.
" Indeed, " he said, " it is too soon for me to get
married, my member is not big enough yet, it
does not reach to my arse. I must wait a year
or two. " The time passed, and the fool thought
only of lengthening his member. At last he succeeded; his member not only reached to his
arse but passed it. " Now, " said the young
man, " I can marry without shame. I have
enough to satisfy my wife, and she will have no
need to go with other men. " What sense can you
expect from a fool? thought his father to himself, and he answered the young man; " Very
well, my son, since your member has grown
so that it reaches your arse, all you have to do
is to marry yourself; remain a bachelor, con-
tinue to live here, and roger yourself with your
own tool. " — So ends the story.

XIII

The pike's head.

A young peasant girl went one day to harrow
in her father's field. She had worked some time,

when she was called home to eat some fritters. She left the horse and the harrow in the field. " As I am coming back, they may as well stay there, " she thought to herself. But the neighbor had a son who was a fool. For a long time past this youth had had his eye on the girl, but did not know how to accomplish his ends. Seeing the horse and the harrow, he jumped over the hedge, unharnessed the animal, and led it into his field; the harrow he let alone, but he pushed the shafts through the hedge, and put the horse in the thills again.

Great was the surprise of the girl, when she came back to the field. " What is the meaning of this? The harrow is on one side of the hedge, and the horse on the other. " She began to whip the poor horse. " What the devil are you doing there? You got out of the field, you must get in again; come over, quick. " The young man heard her and laughed. " If you like, I will help you, " he said, " only, in return allow me to... " " Very well, " replied the cunning girl. She had noticed, on the ground, the head of a dead pike, with its mouth gaping wide open; she picked it up, and hid it in her sleeve. " I will not come to you, " she said to the young man, " nor must you come over here, for fear somebody should see us. Pass your affair through the hedge, and I will put it you know where. " The young man hastened to do as she said;

the girl took the pike's head, opened the jaws, and placed the head on the object he presented to her. Feeling a severe pain, the young man pulled away his member all bleeding, and ran away home, and sat down in a corner. " Confound the girl, " he said, " her... bites most terribly. I only hope my wounds will heal. Never again will I go after a girl. "

Some time afterwards the parents of this youth thought of marrying him; they betrothed him to the neighbor's daughter, and the marriage took place. One day, two days, three days passed, then a week, two weeks, three weeks : and the young man was still afraid to touch his wife. About this time the couple went to see the bride's mother. During the journey, the young woman said to her husband. " Listen to me, my dear Daniouchka. Why, as you have married me, do you never have connection with me? If you cannot do it, what need was there to make my life miserable? " " No, " replied Damilo, " you will not catch me again. Your slit bites. You made me smart so much then, that I thought I should never be cured. " " You are joking, " she replied; " then I served you a trick, but now you need not be afraid. Go on; try here, in the sledge; you will find it nice. " Excited by these words, the young man tucked up his wife's gown. " Wait a bit, Varioukha ", he said: " let me first tie your legs; and then if it begins to

bite, I can get away. " With that he undid the
reins, and knotted them round the naked thighs
of Varioukha. He was a fine strong man, and
he assailed her with such violence, that she uttered loud cries. The horse was a young one; he
took fright and started off at full gallop ; Danilo
rolled out on the ground, and Varioukha, carried away at full speed, arrived, with her thighs
still naked, in her mother's courtyard.

The old woman was looking out of the window ;
she recognised her son-in-law's sledge. " No
doubt, " she said, " he has brought some beef
for the feast. " She went out, and found it was
her daughter. " Oh, mother, " cried the young
woman, " untie me quickly, that no one may see
me in this condition. " When she was untied,
the old woman began to question her. " Where
is your husband? " " The horse threw him out
of the sledge. "

They entered the *izba*, and looking through
the window, they saw Danilo coming. The
children were playing at knuckle-bones in the
court; he approached them, then stopped, and
looked around. The mistress sent her eldest
daughter to bring him to the house. The girl
came to her brother-in-law. " Good day, Danilo
Ivanitch, " she began. " Good day. " " Come into
the house, we are only waiting for you. " " Is
Varvara here? " " Yes. " " Is she still bleeding! "
The girl spat at him, and went away. The old

woman then sent out her daughter-in-law to
welcome the visitor. " Come along, Daniouchka, " she said; " the blood has long since
stopped. " She led him to the house, where he
was received by his mother-in-law, who said to
him, " You are welcome, my dear son-in-law. "
" Is Varvara here? " he asked. " Yes. " " Is she
still bleeding. " " That is finished, long ago. "
At these words Danilo pulled his member out of
his trousers, showed it to his mother - in - law,
and said : " Look, *matouchka*, I buried all that
dagger in her body. " " Come along, come
along; sit down, it is dinner-time. " They sat at
table and everyone began to eat and drink. An
omelette was brought in, and the fool wanted it
all to himself, so he hit on an ingenious strate-
gem. He pulled out his yard, hit it on the top
with his spoon, and said, " Look here; the whole
of this dagger has been in Varioukha's body. "
and then he began to cut the omelette with his
spoon. Naturally, all the guests left the table ;
Danilo ate up all the omelette ; after which he
thanked his mother-in-law for her hospitality.

XIV

An unfortunate marriage.

A Cossack couple had a son called Gritzko ;
and whilst he was minding the sheep on the

steppes, his father and mother talked about him. " Old woman, we must marry Gritzko. " " All right, let him be married. " The parents sent for their son. " Good day, *panotche* (1), " said the servant who was sent to fetch him, " your father wants to see you. " Having arrived at the house, the young man found the two old people, who welcomed him with these words: " Good day, my son, how are you ? " " Thank God I am fairly well, papa and mamma; but why have you sent for me? " " Look here, " said the father, " your mother and I are now old, and you must get married. " " I won't. I will go back to the steppes. " " Wait a bit; don't be frightened; we will consult some worthy people and hear what they say. " " Very good. " The worthy people were consulted and advised the parents to give their son six sacks of corn, and send him to the market. " Instruct him, " they said, " not to sell it either to the Jews, nor the merchants, nor old women; but he is to sell it only to young girls, and to ask for a grind as the price of a sack. "

When he returned home, the old Cossack said to his son, "Gritzko, take oxen, yoke them to the cart, and take six sacks of corn to the market; only you are not to sell it to Jews, nor merchants,

(1) Son of a *pan* or gentleman, a polite expression used in the Ukraine when addressing a young man.

nor old women; sell it to young girls. " The lad
put to the oxen, placed six sacks of corn in the
cart, and went to the town. On coming near the
market, he met a Jew, who said, " Good day,
panotche, what have you to sell? " " Nothing
at all, Jew. " The young man was then accosted
by a merchant. " What have you to sell, *panotche* ? " " Nothing at all. " Then a young girl
passed, and asked the same question, " What
have you to sell? " " Corn, " he replied. " How
much have you! " " Six sacks, " " And what are
you asking for that! " " A grind. " " Can't you
take less? " asked the girl, surprised at such a
demand. " No; that's the lowest price. If you
give me a grind, I will give you my corn. "
" Bring your sacks to my house. " They set
out. When they came to the door of the house,
Gritzko asked where he should put the sacks.
The girl showed him the place, went into the
house, prepared a repast and then called the
young man. " Come here, *panotche*. " He came
to her. " Very well, *panotche*, do with me what
you like. " Gritzko soon profited by this permission, and when he had satisfied his passion, he
thanked the girl for her kindness. She replied,
" Thank the Holy Father. "

When the lad arrived home, his parents asked
him, " Have you sold the corn, my son ? " " I
have sold it. " " For what price ? " " For a
grind. " " Did you find that nice, my son ? "

" Better than I can describe. " " Very good, my
son; get married and you can have that pleasure
with your wife. " " If that is the case I am ready
to be married. " " All right, old woman, " said

the father, " God be praised, our Gritzko con-
sents to be married. " The old couple sent a
" matrimonial agent " to a rich peasant. " May
God aid you! " said this woman as she entered
the *izba*. " Good day, grandmother. " " What

good news have you today ? " " I have a purchaser for your merchandise. " The " agent "
at once obtained for Gritzko the hand of Gapka,
the daughter of the *moujik*. A groom's man
was chosen, the friends were invited, they went
to the church, the marriage was celebrated, and
the rest of the day was spent in feasting. Then
the couple was conducted to the bridal chamber.
" Listen to me, Gritzko, " said the groom's man
to the newly-married husband, " do you know
where to futter ? " " Why should I not know ? "
" Well, where is it ? " " On the bed. " " No,
you are joking, it is where the hair is. " " Very
good. " The guests left the newly-married couple
alone together, and returned to finish the feast.
When he had been lying some time with Gapka,
Gritzko wanted to futter. He began to feel about
the furniture and on the shelves, but he could not
find what he sought. In the room was a bracket,
very high up, and on this was hung a brush.
Seeing this, Gritzko climbed on the bracket,
stretched out his arm, and began to feel the
brush. " No, " said he, " there is nothing there to
futter. " But he was afraid to get down from the
bracket. The groom's man came to wake up the
couple. " Good day, young Gritzko, " said he, as
he knocked at the door. " Good day, " replied
Gritzko who was still sitting astride on the
bracket. " Well, Gritzko, did you find the
hair? " " Yes. " " Did you mount on it? "

" Yes; and the devil of it is I am there still. "
" Let go and tumble off. " The young man
obeyed this advice, and, in falling, hurt his
head, and made it bleed. " Well, " said the
groom's man, " have you slipped off? " " Yes. "
" Does it bleed? " " Certainly it does. Open the
door! " As soon as the door was opened, Gritzko
rushed out of the house, and ran towards the
steppes where his sheep were pastured. As he
passed before the court of the *pope's* house,
the dogs ran out at him. The young man ran
away, and took refuge in the church, which was
full of people, for it was a Sunday. " What a
lot of people the dogs have caused to take refuge
here, " thought Gritzko, surprised to see such
a crowd. " They are talking in a low voice, and
they are saluting; what does that mean ? " Soon
he saw the *pope* clad in a gold chasuble. The
priest advanced bowing, and accompanied by a
large procession. He came near Gritzko. " What
is this ? " said the latter to himself: " he is
throwing fire on the people. " Finding the *pope*
close to him, Gritzko said, " Gently, *batko*, do
not burn my eyes. " The *pope* did not appear
to have heard these words. Then the young man
pushed him so violently that he fell on the
ground, and, directly, fifty people assailed the
fool. He managed to get out of their hands,
and fled to the steppes, much astonished at having
had to defend himself against people, who, just

before, had been prodigal in their salutations to him.

Gapka, however, felt sad without her little man, and wept. She was advised to go and find Gritzko on the steppes, where he was minding his sheep by the side of a pond. " You will say to him: " Can one bathe here, my little man ? " and he will reply, " Why not ? You can bathe very well ! " You must say, " But perhaps the water is very deep, you get in first, " and then the affair will be settled.

Gapka went to the steppes. " Good morning, *panotche*, " she said when she met Gritzko close to the pond. " Good morning, " he replied. " Can I bathe here, my little man ? " she asked. " Why should you not? " — " But perhaps the pond is very deep; you set me the example. " At this Gritzko pulled off his shirt and trousers, and walked into the pond. " You see, " he said, " it is only up to my knees. " Gapka, in her turn, undressed and walked into the pond. " What is that? " she asked, fixing her eyes on the tool of the young man. " A roll of tobacco, " he replied. " What is it for? What do you do with it ? " " I piss. " " And what do you give it to eat? " — " Why, nothing. " " That is why it is so thin. " Gritzko, on his side, had noticed Gapka's slit and asked, " And what is that you have there ? " " A pouch. " " What is the use of it ? " " To hold tobacco. Put yours into it

and try. " " Oh, it would bite me. I am afraid. "
" No, it shall not bite you. " After a little
hesitation, the lad consented to put his tobacco
into Gapka's pouch, and she helped him as
much as she could. Gritzko was very pleased
with the operation, so he left the steppes very
soon, and ran home. " Papa ! Mamma ! " he
cried, as soon as he had entered the house ;
" where is my wife ? " " Why do you want
her? " " I want to futter her. " " She will
come. " The young woman was well pleased,
nevertheless she said to her husband, " Wait till
after dinner, my mother has made some fritters. "
—" No, I am not hungry, " replied Gritzko,
" let us put the tobacco into the pouch " — and
from words he quickly proceeded to deeds.

A little while afterwards Gapka complained of
feeling ill. " What shall I do ?" asked the young
man. " Good old people have told me, " she
replied, " that if our neighbor's ox licks my
arse, that would perhaps cure me; go and ask
him to lend it. " Gritzko went to the neighbor's house. " Can your ox come and lick my
wife's arse? " — " Certainly. " He came home and
told Gapka : " The neighbor is going to bring his
ox. " The young woman tucked up her clothes,
backside exposed and, whilst her husband sup-
ported her, Ivachka, the neighbor's son, with
whom she had previously agreed on the matter,

drove away the fever by means of a remedy
you can easily guess. " Well, how are you ? "
asked Gritzko. — " I feel rather relieved. "

A little time afterwards, Gritzko himself felt
ill. " Wife, " he said, " go and ask the neighbor to let his ox come and lick my arse. " Gapka
soon came back with the animal. " Come, and put
yourself in the proper position at the window. "
Gritzko took off his trousers, but, no sooner had
he presented his posterior that the ox tossed
him in the air with its horns.

XV

A timorous young girl.

Two young peasant girls were talking together. " I am like you, my dear. I will never be married. " — " What need is there for us to be married? After all, we are our own mistresses. " — " Have you ever seen, my dear, the instrument they push through us? " — " Yes. " — " Well, is it big? " — " Ah, my child, there are some which are positively as big as a fist. " — " But that is enough to kill us. " — " To give you an idea of the thing will you let me try with this bit of straw? " — The one to whom this proposal was made, lay on the ground, and her friend introduced a straw into her genital parts. — " Oh, that hurts me. "

Some time afterwards, the father of one of the two young girls obliged her to choose a husband. When she had passed two nights in the conjugal bed, the newly-made bride came to see her friend. " Good morning, my dear! " — The other began to load her with questions. " Well, " replied the visitor, " if I had only known what it was like, I should never have obeyed either my father or my mother. I thought really I was about to die, and I can assure you I am not exaggerating. " This speech so frightened the other young woman that she swore she would remain a virgin. " I will never be married, " she said, " unless my father compels me, and uses force, and even in that case I will only marry as a matter of form, and will choose some man who is not completely furnished. "

Now there was in the village a youth who was extremely poor; he was too beggarly to be able to make a good match, and yet he wanted to marry some rich girl. Having overheard the conversation we have just read, this young man resolved to profit by it. " If ever I get a chance to speak to that little fool of a girl, I will tell her that I have no tool, " he decided. It happened one day that as the girl was going to church, she saw this lad who was leading his sorry nag to water. The poor beast stumbled at every step, and looked so starved that the girl laughed to see it. Just at this minute the horse began to ascend a small, steep hill, but it fell and rolled to the bottom. The young man was furious; he seized the animal by the tail, and began to flog it pitilessly. " Get up, or I'll flay you !" he shouted. —" Why do you so ill-treat your mare, you wicked man? " asked the girl. He lifted up the mare's tail, and fixing his eyes on what he there saw, answered, " What am I do with her? I would give her a good futtering, but I have not the wherewithal. "

When she heard these words, the peasant girl

pissed for joy, and said to herself, " That is the
husband the Lord has given me as a reward for
my simplicity. " She returned home, sat in the
corner the farthest away from the door, and
never opened her lips. Every one else sat down
to dinner; they called her, but she replied, as
though vexed, " I am not hungry. " — " What
is the matter, Douniouchka? " asked her mother.
— " Come, come ! Why are you sulking so ?
Perhaps you want to get married? " said the
father in his turn. The girl was thinking only of
marrying the young man who had no yard. —
" If I marry with anyone it will only be with
Ivan; but whether you consent to let me marry
him or not, I will never be the wife of any other
man, " she told her parents. — " What are you
thinking of, you fool? Have you lost your senses?
With him you would be reduced to beggary! "
— " No doubt that will be my fate. But if you
do not let me have him for my husband, I will
throw myself into the water, or hang myself. "

What was to be done? The old man, who until
then, had never allowed this poor devil of an Ivan
to enter his presence, was obliged to go to him
and offer him his daughter's hand. On entering,
he found the young man engaged in cobbling
an old shoe made of bast. " Good morning, Ivanouchka ! " — " Good morning, old man. " —
" What is that you are doing? " — " I am
mending my old shoes. " — " Shoes of bark

bast! you should buy some new boots. " — " It was as much as I could do to get together fifteen kopecks to buy bark bast; how then could I procure boots? " — " But why do you not get married, Vania? " — " Who would give me his daughter in marriage? " — " If you like I will give you mine. Kiss me on the mouth. "

The business was settled. The wedding was celebrated with great pomp, and after a copious repast, the groom's man conducted the young couple to the nuptial chamber, where he left them. Ivan soon showed his wife that there was nothing wanting to him. " Fool and idiot that I am! " thought Dounia, when she had received sensible proofs of her husband's virility. " I have made a nice mess of it! Since this was to happen to me, I might as well have married a rich man! But how did he procure a yard? I must find out that. " And addressing her husband, she said, " Listen to me, Ivanoutchka! Where did you get that yard? " — " I borrowed it for a night from my uncle. " —" Ah, my dear, ask him to lend it you again for another night! "

The following night, the young woman again spoke on the same subject. " Ah, my dear, ask your uncle if he cannot sell you his yard; but make a good bargain. " — " Be it so: I will try to buy it. " He went to his uncle, and gave him a hint how to act, and then returned to his wife. " Well? " she asked. —" What can I say? I have

not been able to arrange it with him. He will not
dispose of it for less than three-hundred rubles,
and that is beyond my means. Where am I to get
such a sum? " — " Very well, ask him to lend
it to you again for a night; tomorrow I will get
the money from my father, and we will buy it
outright. " — " No; you go to him yourself; it
would embarrass me to have to ask again. " —
Dounia went to the uncle; on entering the
izba, she prayed to God, and made a low bow.
" Good morning, my little uncle. "   —" Good
morning. What good news is there? "   —" I am
ashamed, my little uncle, of the errand which
has brought me to you, but there is no good in
hiding it. I have come to beg you to lend your
yard to Ivan for another little night. "

The uncle reflected a minute, then nodded his
head, and said, " I will lend it to him; but he
must take great care of it, as it does not belong
to him. " — " We will be very careful of it, my
little uncle: Look! here is my cross as a pledge!
And tomorrow, without fail, we will buy it. "
— " Very well, then send Ivan to me. " — She
bowed to the ground, and returned home. The
next day she went to her father, and made him
give her three-hundred rubles, and bought
herself a good serviceable yard.

XVI

The hot cock.

A *moujik* had a daughter, who said to him one day, " *Batouchka*, Vanka has asked me to let him futter me. " — " Oh, villain, " replied the father, " why should you let yourself be fut- tered by a stranger? I can do that for you myself. " He took a nail, made it red-hot in the stove, and inserted it in his daughter's coynte so well that she could not piss for three months. A little later Vanka again met the young pea- sant girl, and said to her, " Let me futter you! " — " You are joking, Vanka, you devil. My father futtered me, and so burned my vulva, that I have not been able to piss for three months. " — " Don't be afraid, you fool; my cock is cold. " — " You lie, Vanka, you devil. Give me hold of it, and let me feel. " — " There! feel it. " She took the young man's yard, and cried, " What a lying devil you are! It is hot; put it into water. " Vanka did so, but this gave him a belly-ache, and caused him to let a fart. " How it hisses when the water touches it, " said the peasant girl, " I was sure that it was burning. And you tried to deceive me, you ras- cal. " So Vanka found his loving request refused.

XVII

(This is not a story, but a number of pro-
verbs, of a punning nature, which could not
be translated well here. We have endeavoured
to give some idea of this morceau *in the*
APPENDIX.*)*

XVIII

(Here is inserted a beggars' song, quite devoid
of interest, and which would also be difficult to
translate here, and is therefore thrown in at the
end.)

XIX

Family conversations.

A *moujik* had a wife, a daughter, and two
sons, both of tender years. The mother one day
went to the baths with the children, collected the
dirty linen, and began to wash it. She was
leaning over the trough with her back turned to
the urchins. They looked, and laughed at what
they saw. " Oh, Andriouchka, just look! Mamma
has two slits. " —" What nonsense you talk,

there is but one, only it is divided into two. "
— " Oh, those dirty young devils, " grumbled
the peasant woman, " how knowing they are. "
— She went home, and lay down on the stove
with her daughter and the following conversation took place. " Well, my daughter, " said
the mother, " the time is near when you must
get married; and then you will live with your
husband and not with us. " — " If that is the
case, I will not be married. " — " Go to! You
are foolish. What are you afraid of? So far from
frightening good girls, marriage gives them pleasure. " — " Why ! When you have passed a
night with your husband you will not regret
having left your father and mother for him; he
will seem to you better than honey and sugar. "
—" What is there so good about him, *matouchka*? " — " Oh, how foolish you are ! When
you were little, did you not go to the baths with
your father? " — " Yes, " replied the young
girl. — " Did you notice what your father carried
at the bottom of his belly? " — " Yes, mother. "
— " Well, it is that, that is so nice. " —
" Then, " observed the daughter, " if that peg
were split, so as to make five, it would be better
still. "

On hearing these words, the father, who was
sleeping under the shed, could not restrain his
anger. " Oh, the villains, " he cried, " what are
they talking about? I cannot cut my tool into

little bits to please you. " — The girl, however, began to reflect deeply on the matter. — " One tool is not enough, and two would not go in; the best way would be to twist them together, so that they could both be put in at once. "

XX

The first interview between a lover and his lass.

An old man had a son who had come to full age; and another old man had a daughter of nubile years. They thought of marrying them together. " Look here, Ivanouchka, " said the father of the young man. " I wish to marry you to my neighbor's daughter. Try to meet her, accost her politely, and come to an understanding with her. " — The other old man said to his daughter, " Come, Machourka; I wish to give you in marriage to my neighbor's son. When you meet him, speak kindly to him, and establish friendly relations with him. "

The two young people met in the street, and wished each other good day. " My father has ordered me, Ivanouchka, to make your acquaintance, " began the young girl. — " And mine has laid the same command upon me, " answered the lad. — " How shall we begin? Where do you sleep, Ivanouchka? " — " In the vestibule. " " — And I sleep in the *ambar* (1). Come and see me at night, and we can talk together. " — Ivanouchka kept the appointment and lay down by the side of Machourka. — " Did you pass by the side of the *goummo* (2)? " she asked him. — " Yes. " — " Well, did you see a heap of dung. " — " Yes. " — " I sh...t all that. " — " It is a good heap. " — " What are we to do to come to a good understanding? I must first see if you have a good tool. " —" Look here, " said he, unbuttoning his trousers. " In that respect I am well furnished. " — " But it is too big for me, look how narrow I am. " —" Let me try if it will fit. "

The act suited the words. At first the girl began to cry with all her might. " Oh, it hurts me. How it bites. " — " Don't be afraid; there is not room enough for it; that is why it is so angry. " — " See! I was right when I said there was no room for it. " — " Wait a bit, just now it will be more at its ease. " — When she began to enjoy it, Machourka cried, " Oh, my soul, with such a treasure you could gain much money. " — At last they fell asleep. She woke up in the night, and kissed her lover's backside,

(1) The granary, or store room.
(2) Place where the mill-stones are kept.

thinking it was his face. The young man, who had supped well, broke wind. " Oh, Vanka, " said Machourka, " your breath is contaminated. " (lit. scorbutic).

XXI

The *Moujiks* and the *Barine*.

A *Barine* went one Sunday to mass. Whilst he was praying to God, a *moujik* came, and stood in front of him, and this son of a dog let fly a most fe-

tid stench. *What a rascal! How he stinks!*
thought the *barine*, and he approached the peasant, and having first pulled out a silver ruble,
said to him " Look here, *moujik!* Was it you who
made that terrible stench? " The *moujik*, seeing
a ruble in the gentleman's hand, did not hesitate
to reply, " Yes, *barine*. " — " All right, my
friend, here is a ruble for you. " — The *moujik*
took the money, and said to himself, " Certainly
the *barine* must greatly like that kind of smell.
I must go to the church every Sunday, and stand
by the side of him, and each time I shall get a
ruble. " — The mass being over, the faithful
returned to their homes. The peasant went to his
neighbor, and told him his adventure. " Well,
my friend, " said the latter, " on Sunday next I
will go to the church with you. The two of us will
be able to make even a worse stink, and he will
give us both money. "

The next Sunday, they went together to the
mass, placed themselves in front of the *barine*,
and the church was soon filled with a most horrible stench. " Look here, my children, " said the
barine to them! " was it you who farted so well? "
— " Yes, sir. " — " Very well; I thank you, and
I am sorry I have no money with me at present,
but you shall not lose thereby, my children. When
the mass is over, dine copiously, and then come
to my house and fart away, and I will pay you for
all at once. " — " Very good, *barine*, we will

both come to Your Grace's castle presently. "

The service being finished, the *moujiks* went and dined, and after they had stuffed themselves, they went to the *barine's* castle. But he had prepared for them a present of rods and sticks. On seeing the two peasants appear, he said to them, " Well, my children, have you come to fart? " — " Yes, sir. " — Thank you, thank you! But first of all, my boys, you must take off your clothes, for you are thickly covered, and your clothes would intercept the odor. " — The *moujiks* took off all they had on their bodies, — *sarrau*, waistcoat, trousers, and shirt. Then the *barine* made a sign to his servants; the visitors were seized, laid on the floor, and each received five-hundred blows of the stick on his back. It was with great difficulty that the two peasants could limp home, though they started in such a hurry that they never thought of taking their clothes.

XXII

The intelligent housewife.

An old woman had a daughter who was sluttish, and even filthy, but a man was found fool enough to ask her in marriage and wed her. After she had lived a year at most with him, she had a son. One day she went to visit her mother, who gave her a good meal. " Oh, *matouchka*, how

good your bread is, " said the young woman
whilst she was eating, " mine can hardly be eaten, it
is really like brick. " —" Listen to me, daughter, "
replied the old woman, " you certainly do not
knead the dough well enough, that is why your
bread is not good. Try to knead it till your arse
is quite wet, and your bread will be good. "

The woman returned home, opened the knead-
ing trough, and set to work. After having
kneaded for a long time, she tucked up her gown,
and felt if her arse was wet; then she went on
with her work. For two hours she kneaded, and
kept on smearing her backside with her doughy
hands, but she could not be certain whether her
arse was wet. At last, she tucked up her gown,
and said to her little boy as she showed him her
posterior. " Look if my arse is wet. " The child
looked. " Oh, mother, " he said, " you have two
holes side by side, and they are both all over
dough. " The woman then ceased to knead, and
with that dough she made good bread, but, if
people had known how it had been kneaded, they
would not have touched it.

XXIII

No!

An old *barine* was married to a young and
pretty woman. It happened that this gentleman

had to make a long journey, and fearing that his
wife might frolic with some one, he said to her,
" Listen, my dear! I shall be absent for a long
time. You are not to allow any gentleman to enter
the house, and then they will not be likely to
bother you. This is the best thing to do; whoever
may speak to you, and whatever they may say,
always reply No, and never say anything else ! "

With that, he set off on his journey, and the
lady went to walk in the garden. Whilst she was
thus engaged, an officer passed on horseback
Seeing such a handsome *barinia*, he spoke to her.
" Tell me, if you please, what is the name of this
village. " — " No, " she replied. — " What does
that mean? " thought the officer. To all the questions which were put to her, the lady continued to
reply " No. " But her questioner did not lose his
wits. " So, " he said, " if I dismount, and fasten
my horse to the palings, you will not mind? " —
" No, " replied the lady —" And if I enter your
garden you will not take it in bad part? " —
" No. " — " And if I walk with you, you will not
be angry? " — " No. " — He began to walk by
her side. " And if I take your arm you will not
be angry? " — " No. " — He took her arm. —
" And if I lead you to that arbor, you would not
be dissatisfied ? " —" No. " — He led her
to the arbor. " And if I laid you on the ground,
and lay by your side, you would not object? " —
" No. " — The officer took advantage of the per-

mission, and then he continued, " And if I pulled up your petticoats, that, no doubt, would not arouse your wrath? " — " No. " — He tucked up her petticoats, lifted up her legs, and continued, " And if I f...d you, that would not be disagreeable to you ? " — " No. " Thereupon he copulated with her; then he lay by her side, and a minute later, asked, " Now are you satisfied ? " — " No. " — " Well, if you are not satisfied we must begin again ? " He trussed her again, and repeated his question. " Now are you satisfied ? " — " No. " — This time the officer spat, and went away, and the lady rose and returned to the house.

When the *barine* returned off his journey, he asked his wife. " Is all well at home? " — " No. " — " Why, what is the matter? Has anyone ridden you ? " — " No. " — And ask as he might he could obtain no other reply than " No. " At last the *barine* was compelled to regret having given his wife such instructions.

XXIV

The husband who hatched the eggs.

An idle peasant had married a hard-working woman. All day he lay on the stove, whilst she worked in the fields. One day, the woman went to labor in the fields, whilst her husband stayed at home to prepare the dinner, and feed the chickens, but he did nothing at all. He lay down, and whilst he was asleep a crow carried off all the chickens. Their mother filled the farmyard with her cries of distress, but the *moujik* let her shriek herself hoarse. When the woman returned to the house, she asked, " Where are the chickens? What have you done with them? " — " Oh, little wife, a misfortune has happened. Whilst I was asleep, a crow carried off all the chickens. " " Oh, you lazy dog! Now, you son of a whore, you must sit on the eggs, and hatch them yourself. "

On the morrow, the woman went to the fields, and the *moujik* took the basket containing the eggs, placed them in the loft, then took off his trousers and sat upon the eggs. His wife, who was not devoid of cunning, dressed herself up in a cloak and cap borrowed from an old soldier, and in this disguise, she came to the house, and cried at the top of her voice " Hello, master! Where are you ? " The peasant jumped out of the loft, and in so doing, all the eggs fell on the floor and broke. " What are you doing ? " — " Mister soldier, I am minding the house. " — " Have you no wife ? " — " Yes, but she is at work in the fields. " — " Then why do you stay in the house? " — " I am sitting on the eggs. " — " Oh you are, are you; you son of a bitch, " and with his whip the soldier rained blows on the *moujik's* body. " Don't stop in the house, " continued the pretended soldier, " and sit on eggs, but go and work in the fields. " — " I will do so, *batouchka*. I will work and labor hard, I assure you. " — " You lie, you scoundrel, " and the woman again thrashed her husband, and when she had finished, she lifted up her leg, " Look at this, son of a bitch, " she said. " I have been in the wars, and have been wounded, as you see : Well, do you think my wound will heal ? " The *moujik* examined his wife's slit, and replied, " It will heal over, *batouchka*. "

The peasant woman went away, put on her own clothes, and returned to the house, where she found her husband groaning dismally. " Why are you groaning ? " — " A soldier came just now, and has beaten me black and blue all over with his whip. " — " For what reason ? " — " He wanted me to work. " — " You ought to have been thrashed long ago. I am sorry I was not here. I would have asked him to keep on thrashing you. " — " That would have been difficult for him; he is on his last legs. " — " How is that? " — " He has been in a battle and received a wound between the legs. He showed it to me, and asked if it could be cured. I replied that it would heal up, but the wound is very red, and the hair has grown all around it. " Henceforth, the *moujik* cultivated the ground, and his wife kept the house.

XXV

The hunter and the satyr.

A hunter had long scoured the woods without killing anything, and began to gather hazel nuts, and eat them. There came to him a satyr, who asked for some nuts. The hunter gave him a bullet. The satyr put it into his mouth, but his teeth could not bite it. " I cannot crack it, " he said. " Have you been castrated? " said the hunter. — " No. " —" Well, that is the reason. If you like I will castrate you, and then you will be able to crack nuts. " The satyr consented; and the hunter tightly fixed his genital parts between two aspen branches. " Leave me alone! Leave me alone! I don't want any of your nuts, " the satyr began to cry. — " You are joking; you shall learn how to crack nuts. " The hunter cut out his testicles, then let him go, and offered him a real nut. The satyr cracked it with his teeth. " You see I was right when I told you you would be able to crack them. " Then each went his own

way, but before he left, the satyr said in a mena-
cing tone to the hunter. " All right! When you
light your stove, I will play you a trick."

The hunter returned home, and seated himself
on a bench. " Wife, " he said, " I am tired out.
Light the stove. " The wife went and lighted the
stove, and then she lay down alongside the wall.
There came two satyrs, who began to talk together. " Let us burn down the house, " said one of
them. " No, first look if he has a wound like the
one he gave you. " They looked. " Well, my
friend, his is much larger than yours. See how
big it is; you could put your cap into it. And how
red it is. " And with that they separated, and
each returned to his wood.

XXVI

The peasant and the devil.

A peasant had sowed some turnips. When he thought the time had come to pull them up, he went to the field, but they were not above the ground. " May the devil take you, " the *moujik* cried in his wrath, and he returned home. A month afterwards his wife said to him. " Go, and see if it is time to pull the turnips. " The peasant again went to his field, and this time found it covered with fine turnips; but the moment he began to pull them up a little old man appeared, and cried, " Why are you stealing my turnips? " — " What do you mean by *your* turnips? " " No doubt they are! Did you not give them to me before they were up? I have taken great care of them and watered them. " — " But I sowed them. " " That may be, " said the devil. " You may have sowed them — I do not say you did not, but I watered them. But hold, I will tell you what we will do. We will come here, you and I, each with what equipage we please. If you can guess what I am riding on, the turnips shall be yours; and they shall belong to me if I can guess what you are riding on. The *moujik* agreed to this arrangement.

The next day, he took his wife with him, and when they were near the field, he made her go on all fours, tucked up her petticoats, stuck a carrot into her arse, and covered her face under her long hair. As for the devil, he caught a hare, mounted on it, and on arriving asked the *moujik*: " What did I come here on? " — " What does it eat? " asked the peasant — " The young shoots of the aspen tree. " — " Then it is a hare. " On his side, the devil tried to recognise the animal the peasant was mounted on, and began to walk around it. " The long hair," he observed, " is, of course the tail; and here is the head, but it is eating a carrot. " This completely puzzled the devil, and he confessed himself beaten. The peasant pulled up the turnips, and sold them, and from that day began to prosper.

XXVII

The peasant who did his wife's work.

It was harvest time; and a peasant and his wife went every day to reap their wheat. Every morning, at daybreak, the wife woke up her husband, and he went to the field to work, whilst his wife remained at home to light the stove, do the cooking, and look after the household affairs;

and after that she carried the good man his dinner, and labored with him in the field till the evening. When night fell, the couple returned home, and the next day it was the same thing over again.

At last, the peasant grew tired of his work. One morning, when his wife woke him as usual to go to the field, he refused to get up, and replied with insults. " No, you whore! In the future you will have to go and do the harvesting, and I shall stay at home. Whilst I am reaping down there, you are idling about, and you never come to give me a lift, until I have already had a bellyful of work. " His wife remonstrated, but to all her arguments he only replied, " I won't go. " " To-day, " said she, " is Saturday, and there is a lot to do in the house, the shirts to be washed, the millet to be pounded for the meal, the bread to be baked, the butter to be churned. " — " I will do all that myself, " replied the peasant. " Very well, do it! I will teach you what work is. " So the woman brought a large bundle of dirty linen, then she fetched for her husband the flour to make the bread, the cream to make the butter, the millet to pound for the meal; then, after having told him to keep an eye on the hen and chickens, she took a sickle, and went off to do the harvesting. " I will have another nap, " the peasant decided, and he rolled himself up in the bed-clothes, and slept till dinner-time.

When he woke up at noon, he saw all the
work that his wife had prepared for him, and did
not know where to begin. Finally he took the
shirts, carried them to the brook, and when he
had put them in the water, returned to the house,
saying to himself: " Bah! I will let them soak
for a minute. I will come back and spread them
out presently, and they will dry. " But the
brook was very rapid, and all the shirts were
carried away by the current. Having returned
to the house, the *moujik* put the flour in the
trough, and poured the water on it. " I will let
the flour soak. " Then he put the millet into the
mortar, and began to pound it, but just then he
saw the hen roaming about the porch, and the
chickens all dispersed in different directions.
Very soon he caught them all, and tied them all
together with a string around their legs, and this
string he fastened to the mother's leg, and after
that, he went on pounding the millet. But an idea
struck him that he could also make the butter. He
got the jar containing the cream, and fastened it
on his buttocks. " Like that, " he thought, "whilst
I am pounding the millet, the cream will be
shaken up, and the butter will make itself. "

While he was carrying out this program,
the hen was picking about the yard, dragging
the chickens after it; when suddenly a goshawk
swooped down, seized it in its talons, and carried it off with all the chickens. Hearing the cries

of the luckless family, the *moujik* ran out of
the *izba*, but in his hurry, the jar was knocked
against the door, and broke, and all the cream
was spilt on the ground. Thinking only of helping
the hen, the peasant forgot to shut the door of
the house, and the pigs went in, knocked over
the trough, ate up all the dough, and did the
same to the millet. After having vainly tried to
rescue the hen from the claws of the goshawk,
the *moujik* returned and found the *izba* full of
pigs, and in a filthy state. He drove them out
with some difficulty. " What is to be done now? "
he asked himself. " When my wife comes
back she will be furious! I have made a nice
mess of it and no mistake. Never mind! I will go
and fetch the shirts which are soaking in the
brook. " He harnessed the mare, and took the
cart down to the brook, but though he cast his
eyes in every direction, the linen had disappeared. " I must look in the brook, " he undressed,
took off his shirt and trousers, and went into the
brook, but his search was useless. Tired out at
last, he regained the bank, but he could not
find either his shirt or trousers; some one had
taken them. What was to done? It was impossible to dress himself and he could not return to
the village naked; " I will pull up some tall
grass, " he said to himself, " and cover up my
c...k; then I will get into the cart and return
to the house. Like that I shall look less inde-

cent. " He pulled up some grass, and made a
kind of little apron. The grass looked tempting to the horse, which made a huge bite, and
gobbled it up, and did not even spare the *moujik's* genital parts. He began to utter horrible
cries. However, somehow or other, he got back
to the house, and went and sat in a corner.

" Well, have you done all the work? " asked
his better half, when she returned. — " Yes,
dear wife. " — " Then where are the shirts? "
— " They were carried away by the brook. "
" And the hen and chickens? " " A goshawk took
them. " — " And the dough? And the millet? "
" The pigs ate them. "—" And the cream? "—" I
spilt it all on the ground. " — " And your c...k;
where is that? " — " The mare has swallowed
it. " " Oh, you son of a dog, a nice mess you
have made of it all. "

XXVIII

The blind man's wife.

A gentleman became blind, and his wife took
advantage of his infirmity to deceive him with a
lawyer's clerk. The idea occurred to the husband
that his wife committed adultery, and from that
time he kept close to her skirts. What could she
do? One day when the husband and wife were in
the garden, the clerk came there also. The wo-

man was amorous, and whilst the gentleman was sitting under an apple-tree, she abandoned herself to her lover. A neighbor, whose windows overlooked the garden, was a witness to this scene, and said to his wife, " Just look, my dear, at what is going on near that apple - tree. Suppose that at this moment, God should open the eyes of the blind man, and he should see that, what would happen? No doubt he would kill her. " — " Make your mind easy, my friend, the wanton would find means to get out of the scrape. " — " Why, what means could she find? " — " Oh, you would see if the case were to occur. "

It happened that the Lord allowed the blind gentleman to recover his sight, just at the moment when his marital honor was receiving this wrong. He surprised the guilty parties in the very act, and began to cry out. " Oh, you hussy!

What are you doing, you cursed whore? " —
" Oh, how glad I am, my dear, " replied the
lady; " Do you know, last night I heard a voice
which said to me. 'If you commit adultery with
such and such a lawyer's clerk, the Lord will
open your husband's eyes.' The prophecy has
come true. Thanks to me, God has restored your
sight. "

XXIX

The grouse.

A hunter had searched the woods for two days
without killing anything. The third day, he made
a vow, " Whatever I may kill I will give it for
a flutter with a woman. " Then he returned to
the wood, saw a grouse, and killed it. As the hunter was returning home with his game, a lady
saw him from the window of her house, and invited him to enter. " What is the price of that
grouse? " she asked — " It is not for sale: I
have made a vow concerning it. " — " What is
that? " — " When I went hunting today I made
a vow that I would give whatever I killed for a
flutter. " — " I do not know what to do, " answered the lady. " I greatly long for that grouse.
Cost what it may, I must have it. But my conscience would not allow me to lie under you. " —

" That is easily settled, madam; I will lie under
you, and you shall be on the top. " — So it was
done. — " Now, *moujik*, give me the grouse. " —
" Why should I give it you? It was not I
who futtered you, but you who futtered me? " To
give up all hope of getting the grouse was more
than the lady could do. " Very well, " she said,
" then you get on me. " — The *moujik* rogered
her a second time. " Now, " said she, "give me
the grouse. " — " Why so ? We are quits, that's
all. " — " Well then, get on me again. " — He
repeated the operation, after which she said, " It
seems to me that I have well earned the grouse
this time, " and though he did it unwillingly,
the hunter was obliged to give her the game, and
return home empty-handed.

XXX

The Bishop's reply

A General and a Bishop were talking together.
" We miserable sinners, " said the first, " cannot
live without offending; we are bound to forni-
cate. How does your Grace manage never to sin? "
— " Send to my house tomorrow, " replied the
Bishop, " and you shall have the reply to that
question. "

On the morrow, the General said to his lackey,

" Go and ask the Bishop to give me the reply he promised me. " The servant went, and a lay brother announced to the Bishop that the General's servant was there. " Let him wait a little, " said the Prelate. One hour, two hours, three hours passed, and the servant still waited. The reply did not come, so he begged the lay brother to remind the Bishop of the object of his visit. " Let him wait a little longer, " replied the Bishop. When the lackey had stood about for a long time, fatigue obliged him to lie down in the ante-chamber; there he went to sleep, and did not wake till the next morning.

He returned to his master, and said: " I remained there till this morning, but he gave me no message for you. " — " Return to him, " were the General's orders, " and insist upon having his reply. " The lackey went again to the Bishop, who this time received him in his cell. " Yesterday did you remain standing? " asked this Holiness. — " Yes. " — " And at last you lay down and went to sleep? " — " Yes. " — " Well, my member does exactly the same thing. It stands for a certain time then it gets tired, and lies down. Tell the General that. "

XXXI

A crop of prickles.

Two peasants went to sow rye, each in his own field. An old man passed and spoke to one of them. " Good day, *moujik!* " — " Good day, old man. " — " What do you sow? " — " Rye, grandfather. " — " Well, may God aid you. May your rye grow tall, and be heavy with grain! " The old man then came to the other peasant. " Good day, *moujik*, " said he. — " Good day, old man. " — " What is it you sow? " — " What business is it of yours? I am sowing prickles. " — " Very good; I wish you a good crop! " The old man went away, the *moujiks* finished their sowing, and went home.

When the spring rains had watered the soil, the rye of the first peasant sprouted well and strong, but in the next field only prickles came up; their red heads covered a whole *desiatine;* you could not put your foot down anywhere for tools! The two peasants came to see if their rye had sprouted. The first experienced great satisfaction at the sight of his field, but the other felt his heart sink within him. " What am I to do with such devils as these? " he thought.

Harvest time came. The two *moujiks* returned to their fields, and the one began to reap his rye;

the other, at the first glance he threw on his field,
saw that the prickles with which it was covered,
had attained a height of an *archine* and a half (1),
and their red heads erect in the air looked like a
field of poppies. After having long gazed at this
spectacle, the peasant returned to his house.
When he got home, the first thing he did was to
take a knife and well sharpen it; he provided
himself also with some paper and twine, and then
he returned to the field. There, he began to cut
all the c...ks, wrapped them two by two in paper,
tied string round each packet, and put them in
his cart to go and sell them in the town. " Yes, "
he said to himself, " I will offer them for sale
there; perhaps some woman will be found fool
enough to buy a couple! "

Whilst he led his cart about the streets of the
town, he cried with all his might, " Who wants
prickles? I have fine prickles to sell; splendid
prickles; fine prickles. " A lady who heard him
crying his wares, said to her young waiting woman, " Go quickly, and ask the *moujik* what he
has to sell. " The girl ran out into the street.
" Hi! *moujik*, what have you to sell? " —
" Prickles, madam. " When she returned to the
house, the girl did not dare to repeat the word to
her mistress. " Speak, you fool, " said the
lady. " There is nothing to be ashamed of!

(1) About 3 feet 6 inches.

What is he selling? " — " Well, madam, the
rascal is selling prickles ! " — " How stupid
you are! Run after him quickly, and ask him
what price he wants for a couple. " The servant-
maid came to the peasant. " How much a couple? " she asked. — " A hundred rubles; that is
the lowest price. " As soon as the servant had
carried this reply to her mistress, the *barinia*
gave her a hundred rubles. " Here, " she said,
" go and choose a couple of good ones; pick
them out long and thick. " The girl took the
money to the peasant. " Only be sure and give
me the best you have, *moujik*. " — " They are
all very fine, " he replied.

The servant-maid took a couple of fine, flou-
rishing tools, and carried them to her mistress.
The lady examined them, and as they greatly
pleased her, she made haste to put them where
they ought to go, but they refused to enter. " Did
not the *moujik* tell you what you ought to say to
make them act? " she asked the servant. —
" He said nothing, madam " — " Oh, what a fool
you are! Go quickly and ask him. " — The girl
went again and found the peasant. " Here, *moujik*; tell me what orders must be given to your
wares to make them act. " — " If you give me
another hundred rubles, I will tell you, " replied
the *moujik*. The servant went, and informed
her mistress of this fresh demand. " He will
not tell you for nothing, madam; he asks for

another hundred rubles. " — " Well! take
him the money! A couple of hundred rubles is
really not dear for a pair of machines like these. "
— The peasant, having received the money, said
to the servant. " When your mistress wants to
use them, she has only to say " *No, no!* " As
soon as this reply had been conveyed to her, the
lady lay upon the bed, lifted up her clothes, and
said " *No, no.* " The two tools immediately performed their duty; but when the *barinia* wished
to make them leave off, she found it impossible.
The situation was becoming distressing; and in
her trouble the poor woman started off the servant again. " Run after that son of a dog, and
ask him what I must say to make them come
out. " The servant ran at full speed, caught up
the *moujik*, and told him her errand. " Tell me,
moujik, what is to be done to make the prickles
leave the body of my mistress, for at present
they are worrying her sadly. " And the peasant
replied : " If she will give me another hundred
rubles I will tell her. " — The girl returned in
all haste to the house. The *barinia* was lying
on the bed, groaning. " Take the hundred rubles, " she ordered, " which still remain in the
drawer, and carry them quickly to that scoundrel. Make haste, for I am at the point of death. "
When the peasant had received the third pay-
ment of a hundred rubles, he told her the word
for which she awaited. " She has but to say

Tprrou! and they will come out at once. " —
The servant maid tore back, and when she
returned to the house, she found her mistress
senseless, with her tongue hanging out of her
mouth. So the servant herself cried " *Tprrou!* "
The two prickles came out. The *barinia* was
cured; she rose, took them, and put them in a
safe place. After that, she led a very pleasant
life: Whenever she liked, she was futtered by
the tools, and it sufficed to say, " *Tprrou* " to
them to get rid of them.

One day, the lady went to see some friends in
the country, and forgot to take the tools with
her. When the evening came, she felt very sorry
not to have them, and prepared to return home.
Her hosts insisted that she should remain till the
next day. " It is absolutely impossible, " she
said; " I have left at home a certain thing
without which I cannot sleep. " — " Oh, well,
if you like, " replied the master of the house we
will send for it, by a trusty servant who will
bring it to you safely. " — The visitor consent-
ted. So a lackey was ordered to saddle a good
horse, and to fetch the article required from the
lady's house. " You will ask my maid for it, "
added the lady; " she knows where it is. "

When the lackey arrived at the *barinia's*
house, the maid gave him the prickles wrapped
up in paper, and he put them in his back pocket,
and remounted his horse to return to his master.

On the road, the horseman had a hill to climb, and as his horse went too slowly, he cried, " No, no ! " Immediately the prickles came out of the

paper, and introduced themselves into the arse of the lackey, who was terribly frightened. " What are these monsters? Where do the cursed things come from? " he said to himself, and he almost burst out crying, for he did not know what would happen. But on descending the hill on the other side, the horse trotted so quickly that the lackey was forced to cry " *Tprrou!* " The same moment

the prickles evacuated the place they had occupied;
the servant took them, wrapped them in paper
again, and arrived at the house, where he handed
them to the *barinia*. " Well, " she asked, " have
you brought them safe and uninjured? " " May
the devil take them, " he replied, " if I had not
had a hill to come down they would have futtered me all along the road (1). "

XXXII

The enchanted ring.

In a certain village there lived three brothers
who did not agree well together, and decided
therefore to divide their property between them.
But the goods were not divided equally; fortune
favored the two eldest, and the youngest had
scarcely anything. All three were bachelors.
One day they all met in the street, and decided
that it was quite time they were married. " You
have the best of it, " — said the youngest to his

(1) In another version of this story the lady sends the
lackey for a box, which he is not to open. He opens the
box, out of curiosity, and when he sees what is inside,
nods his head, and says, *Nou, nou, nou* (Well! well!
well!) of course with the same result as here stated.
Luckily he meets with a wagoner who at that moment
cries *Tprrou* to his horses, and the poor lackey is relieved from his disagreeable situation.

elder brother; " you are rich, and will be able
to marry well; but what am I to do? I am poor,
and my only possession is a tool that comes down
to my knees. "

At this, the daughter of a merchant passed close
to the group of the three brothers. She heard
this part of the conversation, and said to herself,
" Ah, if I could marry that young man. He has
a c . . k that comes down to his knees! " The elder
brothers married, and the younger remained a
bachelor. But when she returned home the merchant's daughter could think of nothing else
but how to obtain him for her husband. Several merchants asked her hand in marriage, but
she refused them all. " I will have no other husband than the young man, " she said. The
parents scolded her soundly. " What are you
dreaming of, you little fool? Be reasonable! Why
do you want to marry a poor peasant ? " —
" Don't disturb yourselves about that, " she
replied, " you will not have to live with him. "
Then she addressed herself to a matrimonial
agent, and sent her to tell the young man to
come and ask for her hand. The agent went to
the peasant's house, and said to him, " Listen to
me, my dear! Why do you loaf about like this?
Go and ask in marriage the daughter of such and
such a merchant. She has loved you for a long
time, and would be glad to marry you! "

On hearing this, the peasant put on a new

sarrau, and a new cap, and went straight off to
see the father of the young girl. The girl no
sooner saw the visitor than she recognised him
as the man who had a tool which came to his
knee. By pleading hard, she obtained from her
parents their consent to her union with the
young man.

When the wedding night came, the bride found
that her husband's tool was not as long as a finger. " Oh, you rascal, " she shouted, " you
boasted of having a tool that came down to your
knee; what have you done with it? " — " Ah,
wife, you know that before our marriage I was
very poor. I had to provide for the expenses of
the wedding, and, as I had nothing else on which
I could raise money, I was forced to put my tool
in pawn. " — " And for how much did you
pledge it? " — " Not a large sum; — only fifty
rubles. " — " Very well. Tomorrow I will go
to my mother and will ask her for the money,
and you must take your tool out of pawn. If
not I will never set foot in your house again. " —
— The next morning, the young woman went to her
mother. " I beg of you, *matouchka,* to give me
fifty rubles; I have great need of it. " — " Why
do you want it? — tell me. " — " Well, mother,
this is the reason. My husband had a tool which
came down to his knees, but on the eve of the
wedding, the poor man was obliged to raise
money on something, and pledged it for fifty

rubles. At present, my husband has a tool which is not as long as a finger; he must positively redeem the old one. " The mother fully understood the necessity, and gave the fifty rubles to her daughter, who carried the money to her husband, and said to him, " Now run quickly and redeem your old tool, for fear others should profit by it. "

The young man took the money and went away very sad, " What shall I do now? " he asked himself. " Where can I procure such a tool for my wife? I will walk as long as the earth will bear me. " He walked for a more or less long time, when he met an old woman. " Good day, grandmother, " — " Good day, good man. Where are you going? " — " Ah, grannie, if you only knew how miserable I am. I do not know where to go. " — " Tell me your woes, my dear; I might be able to remedy them. " — " I dare not tell you. " — Don't be afraid, and don't be ashamed, and speak boldly. " — " Well, grannie, this is the case. I boasted of having a tool down to my knees; the daughter of a merchant heard the words, and married me, but the first night she passed with me she found that my tool was not as long as a finger. Then she was vexed! 'What have you done with your big tool?' she asked me. Thereupon she handed me the money, telling me to go and redeem it, or otherwise she would never set foot in my house.

I know not what will become of me. " — " Give me your money, " said the old woman, " and I will help you in your misfortune. "

The peasant counted down the fifty rubles, and received in exchange a ring. " Here, " said she; " take this ring, and put it only on your nail. " — The lad obeyed, and the same instant his prickle became a foot long. " Well, " said the old woman; " is that long enough? " — " But, grannie, it is still not down to my knee. " — " You have but to put the ring lower, my son. " He slipped the ring down to the middle of his finger, and immediately he had a yard five miles long. — " Oh, grannie, what am I to do? It is a calamity to have a member of that size. " — " Put the ring back to the nail, and your yard will only be a foot long. Now, I expect you will deem that length sufficient. Take care never to let the ring go beyond the nail. "

The young man thanked the old woman, and took the road back to his own house, happy to think that he would not have to appear before his wife unsuccessful. After having walked a long way, he felt the need of taking some refreshment, so he went a little way off the road, seated himself by the side of a brook, took from his wallet some small biscuits, dipped them in the water, and began to eat them. Afterwards he lay upon his back and experimented again with the ring. He placed it on his nail, and his tool stood

in the air a foot high. He slipped the ring down
to the middle of his finger and his yard rose to
the height of five miles. He put back the ring,
and his member recovered the humble propor-
tions it had before. When the young peasant had
amused himself for some time in this fashion,
sleep overcame him, but, before he fell asleep, he
forgot to put the ring back in his pocket, and
left it lying on his breast. A *barine* happened to
pass in his carriage with his wife. Perceiving,
near the road, a *moujik* asleep with a jewel glittering on his breast, the gentleman stopped the
carriage and said to his lackey, " Go, and take
that *moujik's* ring, and bring it to me. " The
servant executed his master's orders, and the
carriage went on again. But the beauty of the
ring attracted the *barine's* attention. " Look
what a beautiful ring, *douchenka,* " he said to
his wife. " Let us see if it will fit me. " He
slipped the ring down to the middle of his finger,
and immediately his yard lengthened, knocked
the coachman off his box, passed over the horses,
and extended five miles in front of the carriage.
At this the *barinia* was in consternation, and
cried to the lackey, " Return quickly to the
peasant, and bring him here. " The lackey ran and
woke up the *moujik,* and said to him, " Go to
my master; make haste. " Meanwhile the peasant
was searching for his ring. " May the devil take
you! You have stolen my ring. " — " Don't look

for it, " replied the servant, " but go to my master; he has your ring, and a fine trouble it has given us. "

The peasant reached the carriage almost at a bound. " Forgive me, " began the gentleman in a supplicating voice; " help me in my misfortune. " — " What will you give me, *barine*? " — " There are a hundred rubles. " — " Give me two-hundred, and I will help you. " The *barine* gave the *moujik* two-hundred rubles, and the latter took off the ring. Immediately the gentleman's tool became as it was before. The carriage drove off, and the peasant returned home (1).

His wife, who was looking through the window, saw him, and ran to meet him. " Well, " she asked, " have you taken it out of pawn? " — " Yes. " — " Show me. " — " Come into the house; I cannot show it you in the street. " As soon as they were indoors, the wife kept on repeating, " Show it! Show it! " He put the ring on his nail and his tool became a foot long. He pulled it out of his trousers, and said, " Look wife. " She began to embrace him. "Is it not better, my little husband, that we should have such a treasure at home than leave it with stran-

(1) In another version of the story the ring slips down the peasant's finger while he is asleep, and his member knocks over a carriage that is passing along the road. The *barine* who is in the carriage buys the ring and tries it on, but being frightened at the effect gives the peasant another hundred rubles to take back the ring.

gers? Make haste, and let us have dinner; then we will go to bed, and try it. " She soon covered the table with plates and bottles. The couple dined, and then went to bed. After the wife had experienced the vigor of the member with which her husband was provided, she did nothing during the next three days but look under her petticoats; she seemed to always feel it between her legs. She went to see her mother, and during that time the *moujik* went to sleep under an apple-tree in the garden. " Well, " said the old woman to her daughter, " have you taken the tool out of pawn ? " — " Yes, " replied the young woman, and she entered into long details on the subject.

On hearing this, the merchant's wife was seized with the idea that she would take advantage of her daughter's visit, go to her son-in-law's house, and try for herself this splendid instrument. She managed to slip away quietly, and ran to the peasant's house, where she saw him lying asleep in the garden. The ring was on his nail, and his yard was standing a foot high. " I will perch myself on his yard, " said the mother-in-law at this sight. She soon did so. Unfortunately for her, the ring which the sleeper wore on his nail slipped down to the middle of the finger, and the merchant's wife was suddenly raised five miles high by the rapid elongation of the prickle; the daughter, however, having remarked the absence of her mother, and suspecting the cause, returned home quickly. No one was in the house; she went into the garden, and what a spectacle met her gaze! Her husband was asleep, his yard was

standing in the air, and on the top of it, barely visible was the merchant's wife, being turned about by the wind, like a weathercock.

What was to be done? How was she to rescue her mother from such a dangerous position? A crowd soon formed, and everyone gave his opinion as to how a rescue was to effected. " There is only one thing to be done, " said some: " take a hatchet, and cut the yard. " — " No, " replied others, " you must not do that, or you will kill both persons. If we cut the yard, the woman will tumble to the ground, and break all her limbs. It would be better for us all to pray to God, and perhaps he will perform a miracle and save the old woman. "

Whilst this discussion was going on, the sleeper awoke, and perceived that the ring was in the middle of his finger, and his tool was standing perpendicularly five miles high, whilst some weight pressed him to the ground so much that he could not even turn over on his side. Very gently he slipped back the ring. His yard diminished little by little, and when it was only a foot long, the peasant remarked that his mother-in-law was perched on the end of it. " What brings you there, *matouchka*? " he asked. — " Forgive me, my dear son-in-law: I will never do it again. "

ANOTHER VERSION (1)

There was once a tailor who possessed a magic ring: As soon as he put it on his finger his tool

(1) In another version the man is asleep in the house, and the sudden elongation of his yard carries the mother-in-law clean through the roof.

acquired an extraordinary development. He chanced to be working at a lady's house, and, as he was a very gay and facetious kind of man, when he went to sleep, he always neglected to cover his genital parts. The lady remarked that he had a very big tool and being desirous of tasting the power of such a weapon, she called the tailor into her chamber. " Will you, " she said, " commit fornication with me? " — " Why not, madam? Only there is one condition. You must not fart! If you fart, you must give me three-hundred rubles. " — " Very well, " she replied. They went to bed, and the lady took every precaution possible to prevent farting during the copulation. She ordered her waiting woman to fetch a large onion, to stuff it up her arse, and to hold it there with both hands. These instructions were exactly followed, but at the first assault the tailor made on the lady, the onion was violently expelled, and struck the waiting woman with such force that it killed her stone dead! The lady lost the three-hundred rubles. The tailor pocketed the money, and set off to return home.

After having walked a long way, he felt in need of repose, and lay down in a field; he put the ring on his finger, and his yard became three-quarters of a mile long. As he was thus lying down, sleep overcame him, and whilst he slept there came seven hungry wolves who

devoured the greater part of his tool. He awoke
as though there was nothing the matter, took
the ring from his finger, put it in his pocket, and
continued his journey.

When evening came, the tailor entered in a peasant's house to pass the night. This *moujik* was
married to a young woman who was very fond
of " well-furnished " men. The traveller lay
down in the court, and left his tool visible.
When she saw it, the peasant's wife became quite
excited; she pulled up her gown, and placed
herself on the top of the tailor. " Very good, "
said he to himself; then he passed the ring to the
middle of his finger, and his yard rose little by
little till it was more than half-a-mile high.
When the woman found herself at such a distance from the ground, she lost all wish for
pleasure, and held on with both hands to this
strange support. Her neighbours and acquaint-
ances, who saw in what danger the woman was,
began to celebrate a religious service and pray
for her rescue. But the tailor gently withdrew
the ring from his finger, and the dimensions of
his member began to gradually decrease, and
when it was only a few feet high, the woman
jumped to the ground. " Oh, you insatiable
coynte, " said the tailor to her; " It would have
caused your death if they had cut off my tool. "

XXXIII

The excitable lady.

In a certain kingdom there lived a rich peasant who had a son called Ivan. " Why do you never do any work, my son? " said his father to him. — " It is not yet too late. Give me a hundred rubles, and wish good luck to my enterprise. " — The father gave him the money for which he asked, and Ivan went to the town. In passing near a lordly dwelling, he saw a very handsome lady in the garden. He stopped, and looked at her through the palings. " What are you doing there, young man? " asked the lady. — " I was lost in contemplation of you, madam; you are so beautiful. If you will show me your feet up to your ankles, I will give you a hundred rubles. " — " Why should I not show them? Here, look. " So saying, she raised her dress a little. The young man gave her the hundred rubles and returned home.

" Well, my son, " asked the father, " what business have you done? How have you employed the hundred rubles ? " — " I have bought a bit of land, and the wood to build a shop. Give me two-hundred rubles more in order that I may pay the carpenters for their work. " The father gave the required sum, and

the son returned, and once more stationed himself in front of the palings of the same garden.
The lady, on seeing him, said, " Why have you
come back, young man? " — " Allow me to
enter the garden, madam, and show me your
knees, and I will give you two-hundred rubles. "
She allowed him to enter the garden, and pulling up her gown, showed him her knees. The
lad counted out the money, bowed to her, and
returned home. When he entered the house, his
father questioned him : " Is everything arranged, my son? " — " Yes, father. Give me three-
hundred rubles that I may buy wares to stock
my shop. "

When his father had complied with this demand
the son again went and stationed himself before
the palings of the garden. The father, however,
said to himself, " Let me go and see what his
business is. " Thereupon he dogged Ivan's footsteps, and placed himself a little distance from the
palings, where he could observe all that passed.
" Why have you come back, young man? "
asked the lady. — " If you will not be angry at
the request, " replied the lad, " allow me to let
my yard play round outside your coynte, and
for that I will give you three-hundred rubles."
— " Agreed. " — She allowed him to enter the
garden, and after she had received the money,
she lay down on the grass. Ivan took off his
trousers, and began to tickle gently with his

member the genital parts of the lady, who soon
became so excited that she cried, " Push it in
the middle. Push it in, I beg! " — But the
young man refused. " I will give you back all
your money, " said the lady. — " I do not want it, "
he answered, and continued as before. — " I have
had from you six-hundred rubles; I will give you
back twelve-hundred, only shove it in the middle. "

The father who was behind the palings, and
an observer of the scene that passed, could not
contain himself any longer. " Accept, my boy, "
he cried out: " little brooks make great rivers. "
On hearing these words, the lady jumped up
quickly, and ran away. The young man remained without a kopeck, and began to abuse his
father for interfering. " What did you want to
come shouting here for, old greybeard? "

XXXIV

Dog-fashion.

In a certain kingdom there lived a gentleman
who had a very beautiful daughter. One day, as
she was taking a walk, followed by a lackey,
this latter thought to himself, " What a choice
morsel she is. There is nothing in the world that
I should like so much as to futter her. if it were

only once. I would give my life for it (1). " He was
so absorbed in these thoughts that he muttered,
without knowing it, " Ah, my beautiful young
lady, if I could only salute you dog fashion! "

The girl heard these words and returned to
the house. When night came, she called the
lackey to her. " Repeat, you rascal," she began,
" what you said whilst I was out for a walk. " —
" I ask your pardon, madam. I only said such and
such a thing. " — " No! as you have wished it,
you must act like a dog, and at once, or I will
tell my papa everything. " Having said this, the
young girl lifted up her gown, and placed herself in the middle of the room with her posterior uncovered, and said to the lackey, " Stoop
down and sniff as the dogs do. " The lackey
obeyed. " Now lick it with your tongue, like the
dogs lick. " — The lackey licked her three times.
" Very good! now run around me. " Ten times
did he have to run around her, then was obliged
to smell her and lick her over again. The
poor young man made a wry face over it, but he
was compelled to obey. " There; that is enough
for the present! That will suffice for the first time, "
said the young girl, " now go to bed and return
tomorrow night. "

The following night she had the lackey fetched
again. " Why did you not come of your own

(1) Or literally, " death would no more affright me. "

accord, rascal? I cannot send and fetch you every
time. It is your place to know what you have to
do. " With that she tucked up her gown, went
down on all fours, and the performance of the
previous evening was repeated. Ten times did the
lackey have to smell, lick, and run round her.
After having amused herself for a long time in
this fashion, the girl finished by taking pity on him.
She lay down on the bed, pulled up her gown in
front, and consented to let him futter her for
once. The lackey took his pleasure with her,
and said to himself, " All right, it doesn't matter. I have been obliged to lick her, it is true,
but I got what I wanted. "

XXXV

The two wives.

Two merchants lived in close friendship. They were both married, and on a certain day, the one said to the other: " Listen to me, friend. Let us try an experiment to ascertain which of our wives loves her husband best. " — " Agreed; but how are we to determine that? " — " In this way. We are about to start for the fair at Makarieff, and whichever of our wives weeps the most at the parting, is the one who most loves her husband. " They made their preparations for departure, and when they took leave of their wives, one woman poured forth torrents of tears, whilst the other was cheerful and light-hearted. The merchants started off for the fair, and after they had travelled thirty miles or so, the one said to the other: " How much your wife loves you, and how she wept when you said farewell! Mine, on the contrary, did nothing but laugh! " — " I have a proposal to make, " replied the other. " At present our wives believe us to be on the road to the fair. Let us return home, and see what our wives are doing in our absence. " " Very good. "

It was night when they returned to the town. They first directed their footsteps to the abode of the merchant whose wife had wept so much at saying farewell, and this is what they saw when they peeped in at the window — the woman in amorous converse with a lover!

The paramour filled a glass with brandy, raised it to his lips, and then presented it to the faithless spouse. " Here, drink, my dear! " She sipped it in her turn, and said: " My dear friend! Now I am all your own. " — " What nonsense, all mine! A good deal still belongs to your husband. "

She replied, as she showed her backside: " That is what belongs to that son of a whore! Nothing but my arse! "

After they had witnessed this scene, the two merchants went to see what the wife who had laughed at her husband's departure was doing, and on looking through the window, they saw a lamp burning before the altar. The merchant's wife was on her knees, and praying fervently. " Oh, Lord, " she said, " grant my husband a safe and happy return. " — " Well, " said one of the merchants, " we have seen enough: now let us go to the fair. "

They went to the fair, and did good business; never had they been so fortunate. When they were on the point of returning home, each thought he would take a present to his wife. The merchant who had found his wife praying brought enough rich brocade to make her a cloak. The other bought some of the same stuff, but only for the arse. " Since the arse is the only thing that belongs to me I shall not want more than half an ell: I don't want my arse to be badly dressed. " On their arrival at home, they gave the presents to their wives. " Why did you buy such a small piece? " angrily asked the guilty wife. — " Remember what you told your lover, you whore. As your arse is the only part of you that belongs to me, I bought only enough to adorn what is my own. Wear this brocade on your arse. "

XXXVI

The modest lady.

There was once a young lady who frequently changed her lackeys; she complained that they were always vulgar and foul-mouthed, and quickly got rid of them. At last came a young man who offered himself as a servant. " Be very careful, my lad, " said the lady. " I do not heed money or wages, but I insist that you shall never pronounce an indecent word. How can people use indecent expressions? "

Some time afterwards, the lady went to visit her estates. On approaching a village, she saw a herd of swine: A boar had mounted on a sow, and was performing so vigorously that the foam was coming out of his mouth. The lady called to the lackey. — " What do you wish, madam? " — " What is that?" — The lackey was not devoid of tact. " That? " he replied. " I can tell you what that is. The one underneath must be some relative — a sister or an aunt; and the one on the top is a brother or a nephew. He is ill and she is carrying him to her house. " " Yes, yes, that is it, " said the lady and began to laugh.

Travelling on, they met with a herd of cattle; and a bull was just leaping on a cow. " Well, what is that? " asked the lady. — "I will tell you what that is. The cow is not strong, and cannot find anything to eat, having browsed on all the herbage around her. That is why, as you see, the bull is pushing her towards some fresh grass. " — " That is exactly it, " observed the lady, laughing again.

Next, they passed a drove of horses, and a stallion was serving a mare. " And what is that? " — " Do you see, madam, beyond the wood there is some smoke! No doubt there is a fire somewhere, and the horse has mounted on the mare to ge a better view of the conflagration. " — " Yes, yes, that is true, " said the young woman laughing fit to kill herself.

They arrived at a brook. The *barinia* was desirous of taking a bath, so she stopped the carriage, undressed, and entered the water. The servant watched her without moving from his place. " If you wish to bathe with me, undress quickly! " The lackey divested himself of his garments, and entered the water, exhibiting on his person the tool which is used to make men. At this sight, his mistress quivered with joy. " Look! what is this that I have here? " she asked, showing her slit. " A well, " he replied. — " Yes, that is true! And what is that hanging from you? " — " That is called a horse. " — " Does your horse drink? " — " Yes, madam; will you allow it to drink at your well? " — " Yes, certainly provided that it only drinks at the entrance, and

does not go to the bottom of the well. " The
lackey followed his instructions, but the lady became excited, and cried, "Make him enter further,
further. Let him thoroughly quench his thirst. "
He therefore enjoyed himself with all his heart,
and both were sorry to leave the water.

XXXVII

The good father.

In a village there lived a jolly old peasant, the
father of two pretty girls, and these girls had
many female friends who used to come and
spend the evening with them. The old man was
very fond of women, and at night when the visitors were asleep, he would creep on tip-toe, pull
up the gown of one of them, and begin to forni-
cate; the girl never said anything, but took it
as a matter of course. Consequently it was not
surprising that the old *moujik* had futtered nearly
all the young girls in the village, his two daughters alone excepted.

It happened that one evening a number of
young peasant girls met at his *izba*; they
laughed and chatted, and then each one returned
home; for the one had to set to work at daybreak, another had not obtained her mother's
permission to sleep out, the father of the third

was ill, and so forth. The old man was snoring in the loft; he had gone to sleep after supper and had not seen the girls depart. In the night he awoke, came down from the loft, and crept on tip-toe to the benches on which the girls usually slept. His eldest daughter was asleep on the *kazenka* (1); he lifted up her gown and began to perform energetically, and she, being but half awake, willingly abandoned herself to the caresses of her father.

The next morning, the old man rose, and asked his wife: " Old woman, at what time did the girls who passed the night here leave? " — " What girls who passed the night here? They all returned home last evening. " — " You are joking? Who was it then that I futtered on the *kazenka*? " — " Who? You know very well. It was your eldest daughter. " The old man began to laugh. " Oh, you daughter of a whore! " he said. — " Why do you use such coarse language, you old devil? " — " Hold your tongue, you old beast. I laughed to think that my daughter is really very expert at the game. " — The youngest girl was seated at a bench, putting on her shoes. " It would be a disgrace, " she remarked, " if my sister did not know how to do that; she is nineteen years old. " — " Yes, that is true. It is time she knew her business. "

(1) A bench near the stove in the huts of the Russian peasants.

XXXVIII

The *pope* who begot a calf.

A *pope* and his wife had for their servant a Cossack named Vanka, who —owing to the avaricious character of the *popadia*, — did not live at all well in his master's house. One day the *pope* went with his man to make hay at a place about seven miles off. They came to the field, set to work, and loaded two carts. Presently a drove of cows approached the hay, so taking a thick stick in his hand the *pope* rushed at the animals, drove them a long way off, and returned, covered with sweat, to where the Cossack was working. They soon finished their work, and set out to return home. Night fell whilst they were on the road. " Vanka, " said the *pope*, " would it not be better to lodge at Gvoyd's house in the next village? He is an honest *moujik*, and his court is covered. " — " Very good, *batouchka*, " replied Vanka.

They came to the village, and asked and obtained permission to lodge at the *moujik's* house. The Cossack entered the *izba*, uttered a prayer, and after having saluted the master of the house, said to him: " Listen, master: When supper is ready, say, 'Sit down, all you who have been baptised.' If you say to the *pope*,

" Sit down, spiritual father, he would be offended and would not sit at the table, for he does not like to be addressed in that way. "

During this time, the *pope* was unharnessing the horses; when he appeared in the *izba*, the peasant ordered his wife to serve the repast, and when all was ready, said, " Come to supper, all you who are baptised. " Everyone took his place at the table, except the *batouchka*, who sat upon a bench, for he expected to receive a special invitation; but was disappointed in his expectations. When supper was finished, the master of the house said to the priest, " Why did you not sit at table with us, father Mikhail? " — " I was not hungry, " replied the *pope*. All went to bed. The peasant led his guests to the *skotnaia* (1), because it was warmer there than in the *izba*. The *pope* lay on the stove, and the Cossack in the loft. Vanka fell asleep at once; as to the *pope*, he would have liked to find something to eat, but there was nothing in the *skotnaia* except a trough with some dough in it. He woke up the Cossack. " What is it you want, *batouchka*? " — " Cossack, I am hungry. " — " Well! Why do you not eat? In the trough there is the same sort of bread there is on the table, " replied Vanka; then he came down from the

(1) A place where the cowherd sleeps, and where in winter, the calves and any sick animals are put, and also where the cows are milked.

loft, tipped up the trough, and said: " There is enough there to satisfy you. " — The *pope* began to gobble up the dough, but Vanka pushed the trough, as though by accident, and spilled all the contents over his master. The *pope*, having satisfied his hunger, lay down, and was soon fast asleep.

During the night a cow calved in the stable. On hearing the animal's lowing, the mistress of the house came. She took the calf, carried it to the *skotnaia*, and put it on the stove by the side of the *pope*; then she retired. A little later the *pope* was awakened by feeling a tongue lick his face. His first proceeding was to awaken Vanka. — " What is it you want now? " asked the Cossack. — " Vanka, there is a calf close to me on the stove, and I don't know how it came there. " — " What is the matter with you? You have brought forth the calf yourself, and you say, ' I don't know how it came there!' " — " But how can that be? " demanded the *pope*. — " Why, this is how it is. Don't you remember that while we were loading the hay, you ran after the cows? So now you have given birth to a calf. " — " Vanka, what shall I do to hide that from my wife's knowledge? " — " Give me three-hundred rubles, and I will manage so that nobody in the world shall know about it. " The *pope* gave the money. " But pay attention to what I tell you," continued the Cossack. " Return

home at once, but steal away quietly and leave
your boots here. You can put on my bark
shoes. ''

As soon as the *pope* had gone, the Cossack
went to the master of the house. '' Oh what an
ass you are! Do you know that your calf has
eaten up the *pope*, and left only his boots?
Come and see. '' The peasant, thoroughly fright-
tened, offered three-hundred rubles to the
Cossack as the price of his silence, and Vanka
promised to hold his tongue. He took the three-
hundred rubles, mounted his horse, and went
after the *pope*. When he overtook him, he
said, '' *Batouchka*, the *moujik* is going to take
the calf to your wife, and tell her that you
are its father. '' More frightened than ever,
the *pope* gave another hundred rubles to the
Cossack.

'' Only, '' he begged, '' arrange this matter for
me. '' — '' Return home, and I will undertake
to prevent all scandal, '' replied Vanka ; and
he returned to the *moujik*, and, said: '' The *pope's*
wife went out of her mind when she heard of the
death of her husband. You will get into a sad
mess. '' The foolish peasant begged the Cossack
to accept another hundred rubles '' Only, '' he
added, '' be sure to deceive the *popadia*, and
don't say a word to any one. '' — '' All right,
all right! '' — replied the Cossack. When he
arrived at the parsonage, Vanka extorted some

more money from the *pope;* after which, he took leave of him, married, and from that day saw his affairs prosper.

XXXIX

The *pope* and the trap.

In a village there lived a *moujik* who was a butcher by trade. He kept his meat in a coach-house, but the dogs and cats used to come there and commit many thefts. The butcher therefore arranged a trap on the sill of the window by which these animals used to enter the coach-house. The *pope's* dog went on a marauding expe-dition, was caught in the trap, and lost his life. The *pope* felt the loss deeply, but as he could not bring the dog to life again, he bought another. " What shall I do, " he said to himself, " to pre-vent this dog from meeting with the fate of the other? " He wanted also to play a trick on the *moujik.* At last an idea came to him; he went to the coach-house, took off his trousers, climbed up to the window, and began to s..t on the trap. But suddenly the spring went, and caught the *pope* by the testicles, so that he uttered loud cries. The *moujik* ran up. " Ah, you son of a whore! " he shouted, " What the devil are you doing there? What a race of idiots these priests are! " A crowd assembled, and they disengaged the *pope* the best way they could, but he expired immediately.

XL

The *pope*, his wife, his daughter, and his man.

A *pope* was about to engage a man-servant. " Take care, *pope*, " was his wife's advice, " not to engage a man who indulges in filthy talk; for we have a marriageable daughter ! " — " Very well, mother. I will pay attention to what you say. " The priest started off in his cart, and met with a young man who was walking along the road. " Good day, *batouchka.* " — " Good day, friend; where are you going? " — " I am seeking a place as man-servant, *batouchka.* " — " And I, my friend, am just looking for a man. Will you enter my service? " — " Willingly, *batouchka.* " — " Only there is one condition. It is essential, my friend, that you abstain from the use of all improper words. " — " *Batouchka,* I have never heard one said since I have been born. " — " Very well; take your place by my side. You are the very man I want. " — A mare was harnessed to the cart; the *pope* lifted up her tail, and pointing with his whip to the mare's vulva, said, " What is that, my friend? " — " That is a coynte, *batouchka.* " — " Ah, my friend, I don't want people who speak so coarsely and vulgarly. You may go where you like (1). "

The young man saw how stupid he had been, but the mischief was done. He got out of the cart, and began to consider how he could play a trick on the *pope.* By taking a cross road he came out in front of the *pope's* cart, which soon overtook him. The young man had turned his

(1) In another version of the story the young man replies: " Above is an arse, and below is a coynte. " — " All right, my friend; get out of my cart and go f..k yourself. I cannot take you to my house. My wife would not let you in, for she mortally detests all people who use filthy words. " There is a flavor of rustic humor about this.

cloak. " Good day, *batouchka* ". — " Good day,
friend; where are you going? " — " The fact is
batouchka, that I am seeking a place as a man-
servant. " — " And I, my friend, am just looking for a man. Come and live with me; but it
is on the condition that you never utter an indecent word. Whichever of us lets fall an obscene
word must pay a hundred rubles to the other.
Is that agreed? " — " So be it, *batouchka*. For
my own part, I cannot bear people who use
such words. " — " Well, so much the better.
Seat yourself by my side, my friend. "

The young man obeyed, and the cart took the
road to the village. When they had gone some
little distance the *pope* lifted up the mare's tail
and pointing to the vulva with the handle of
his whip, said, " What is that, my friend? " —
" That is a prison, *batouchka*. " — " Ah, my
lad, I have found in you the very man I was
seeking. " — On arriving at his house, the *pope*
entered with his companion, pulled up his wife's
gown, and pointing with his finger to her slit,
asked : " And what is that, my friend? " — " I
do not know, *batouchka*. I have never in all my
life seen anything so terrible. " — " Don't be
afraid, my friend. That also is a prison. " Then
he called his daughter, tucked up her gown also,
and bidding the young man look at the charms
displayed, asked, " What is that? " — "A prison,
batouchka. " — " No, my friend, it is a lock-up. "

They sat down to supper, and the repast being finished, went to bed. The man climbed on the stove, took the *pope's* socks, put them on his own yard, and holding it in both hands, began to hallo with all his might. " *Batouchka!* I have caught a thief. Light a candle quickly. " — The *pope* rose hurriedly and ran like a madman across the room. " Don't let him go! Hold him tight," he cried out to the servant. " Never fear; he shall not escape. " The *pope* lighted a candle and approached the stove. Then he saw the young man holding in his hands his yard, wrapped up in a pair of socks. " Here he is, *batouchka.* He has taken back your socks. We must punish the rascal. " — " Have you lost your sense? " roared the *pope.* " No, *batouchka,* but I will have no mercy shown to thieves. Get up, *batouchka,* and we will put the rascal in prison. " The *pope's* wife rose. " Put yourself in position, quickly, " cried the young man. Whether she liked it or not, the *popadia* was forced to obey, and the young man hastened to futter her. At this sight the *pope* was in such a rage that he could not help crying out, " What are you doing, my friend? F..g? — " Ah, *batouchka,* you know what was agreed between as to obscene words. Pay me a hundred rubles. "

The *pope* was obliged to undo his purse strings, but as to the young man he again grabbed hold of his member and began to abuse it.

" That is not enough for you, you scoundrel. I will put you in a still worse prison. Come along, my dove, " he added, addressing the *pope's* daughter: " Open your dungeon. " He put the young girl in the required position, and proceeded to serve her as he had her mother. The mother was indignant. " Don't you see, *batouchka*, " she said angrily to her husband, " that he is f..g our daughter? " — " Hold your tongue, " replied the *pope*. " I have already paid a hundred rubles for you, do you want me to pay over again for her? No! Let him do what he likes, — I shall not say another word! " The young man enjoyed himself to his heart's content with the girl, after which the *pope* turned him out of doors.

XLI

The sucking-pig.

In a certain village there lived a *pope* — a very stupid man — who had a daughter so beautiful that it was a pleasure to look at her. The *pope* had also a man-servant, a strong lad. When he had been about three months in the *pope's* service, a child was born to the wife of a rich peasant. The peasant invited the *pope* to come and baptise the newly-born child, and assist at the repast which is given on such occasions. " And I beg of you, *batouchka,* " he added, " to also bring your wife. Priests, it is well-known, like to regale themselves at another man's table. " The *pope* therefore harnessed his horse to the cart, and started off with his wife, leaving his daughter at home with the serving man. He was hungry, and there were in the house two sucking-pigs which the *popadia* had cooked. " Listen to what I am about to tell you, " said the man addressing his master's daughter. " We will eat these sucking-pigs whilst we are alone. " — " So be it. " — He brought one of the sucking-pigs, and he and the young girl ate it. " As to the other, " he said; " I will hide it under your gown, so that it shall not be found, and a little later we will eat it also. If the *pope* and the

popadia question us about these sucking-pigs,
we will both reply that the cat has eaten them. "
— " But how will you hide it under my gown? "
— " That is not your business. I know how. "
— " Very well; hide it. " He ordered the young
girl to stoop down, tucked up her dress, and put
his yard into her slit. " Ah, you hide it very
well, " she said, "but how shall I get it out of
there? " — " Be easy. You have only to show it
some hay, and it will come out of its own
accord. "

In short, the servant-man trussed the *pope's*
daughter so well, that she became pregnant; her
belly began to swell and every minute she was
going into the court-yard. The child moved about
in her womb, and she thought it was the sucking-
pig. She stood on the door steps, lifted up her
leg, and spreading some hay on the ground, called
" *Tchoukh, tchoukh, tchoukh!* " " It will come
out, perhaps, " she thought, " If I call it thus. "

One day, the *pope* noticed her condition, and
had a conversation with his wife on the subject.
" Our daughter is in the family way; ask her
what rascal has managed to seduce her. " The
parents called their daughter; " Annouchka,
come here! What is the matter with you? Why
are you so heavy? " She looked at her father and
mother, but did not reply. " What are they asking
me? " she thought. — " Come; speak! How is it
that you are pregnant? " — The young girl was

still silent. " Answer, you fool! How do you
come to have such a big paunch? " — " Oh,
mamma, I have a little pig in my belly; it was
the serving man who put it there. " At these
words, the *pope* struck his forehead, and dashed
out to look for the man, but he had taken care to
disappear from the house.

XLII

The spiritual father.

It was Lent time; a peasant came to confess.
He put in a bag a billet of birch-wood, tied the
bag up with string, and went to the *pope*. " Well;
speak, my friend! What sins have you committed?
But what have you there? " — " It is a white
sausage that I have brought you, *batouchka*. "
— " Ah, so much the better! It is frozen, I sup-

pose? " — " Yes, it has been in my cellar all the
time. " — " Never mind; it will thaw. " — " I
have come to confess, *batouchka*. Once when I
was at the mass, I fizzled. " — " Is that a sin?
Why, one day it happened to me to f..t at the
altar. That is nothing, friend. Go, and may God
help you. " Then the *pope* undid the string which
fastened the bag, and saw that it only contained
a billet of birch-wood. " Oh, cursed fizzler!
where is the white sausage? " — " Don't you
want a tool, you old farter? "

XLIII

The *pope* and the peasant.

In a certain country — to tell the truth,
in the country in which we live — there dwelt
a *moujik* who was married to a young wife.
The peasant went to do some work a long distance off; leaving his wife, who was pregnant,
at home. The *pope*, who had long lusted after
her, resolved to possess her by a trick. One day,
the woman came to confess to him. " Good day,
Marina," said the priest. " Where is your husband
now? " " He is at work a long distance from
here, *batouchka*. " — " Oh, the rascal, how
could he leave you in such a position. He has put
you in the family way, but he has not finished

his work. At present, you will bring forth a
monster — a child without arms or legs — and
every one in the country side will point the finger of scorn at you."

The peasant woman was very simple. " What
is to be done, *batouchka*? Cannot you help me in
my misfortune? " — " I will try to remedy it —
but is only for your sake, for I would not do
anything for your husband, at any price. " —
" Do try to remedy it, *batouchka*, " implored the
woman, with tears in her eyes. — " Well! So be
it! I will complete your child for you. Come to
my coach-house this evening. I must go there to
get some fodder for the cattle, and I will attend
to your business. " — " Thank you, *batouchka*! "

The peasant woman came in the evening to
the *pope's* coach-house. " Come, my dear, lie
down on the straw. " She lay down and opened
her legs, and the *pope* futtered her six times.
Then he said: " Return home, and may God aid
you. Now all will be well. " The woman thanked
the *pope* profusely for his kindness, and went
away to her own house.

When the *moujik* returned home, his wife
received him with most sullen looks. " Why do
you look so sulky? " he asked. — " Oh, leave
me alone! You can never do anything properly.
You left home without finishing the baby! Luckily the *pope* took pity on me and put the last
touch, or I should have given birth to a mons-

ter. " The *moujik* saw that he had been cuckold-
ed by the *pope*. " Wait a bit! " he thought,
" and I will have my revenge. "

When the time came, the peasant's wife gave
birth to a boy. The husband went to the *pope*,
and begged him to come and baptise the newly-
born child. The priest duly performed the cere-
mony; then he sat down to table, and he found
the brandy excellent. " How good it is, " he said
to the master of the house. " " You ought to
send for my wife, she would be glad to taste it
also. " — " I will go and fetch her myself, *batouchka* " — " Go, my friend. "

The peasant went and invited the *popadia*.
" Thank you for having thought of me. I will
dress myself at once, " she replied. She began her
toilet, and placed on a bench a pair of gold earrings, which she had taken out before she washed
her face. Taking advantage of a moment when
her face was hidden in the towel, the *moujik*
snatched up the earrings and concealed them.
When she had finished washing, the *popadia*
looked for the earrings, but could not find them.
" Have you taken them, *moujik*? " she asked the
peasant. " How could I possibly take them,
matouchka? I saw them disappear, but I must
not tell you what became of them. " — " No
matter; tell me. " — " You were seated on the
bench, *matouchka*, and your coynte swallowed
them. " — " Could you not get them out again? "

— Maybe I could. To please you I will try! "
He trussed her, futtered her twice, and then put
one of the earrings on the end of his yard.
" Here, look *matouchka*. I have found one. " —

After two more operations of the same kind, the
other earring was also found. — " You have
given yourself a deal of trouble, poor man, "
said the *popadia*, but I have another favor to
ask you. Two years ago we lost a copper pot;

try if that is there also. " The peasant performed upon her twice more. " No, *matouchka*, it is
impossible to get it. The pot is there, but it is
turned upside down, and there is nothing to lay
hold of. "

This business being finished, the peasant returned home accompanied by the *pope's* wife.
When she took her place at the table, she said to
her husband: " Well, *batouchka*, I am sure you
must have been waiting for us a long time. " —
" I should think so, " replied the *pope*. " You, "
he added addressing the *moujik*, " would be a
good sort of man to go and seek death. " —
" How could we help it, *batouchka*. My earrings
were lost. I placed them on a bench; then I sat
down there, and my coynte swallowed them.
Very fortunately the *moujik* found them again
for me. " — These words showed the *pope* that
the peasant had paid him back in his own coin,
and you may guess how pleased he was at the
news.

ANOTHER VERSION

A *moujik* was obliged to undertake a journey
to Moscow. He was sorry to have to go whilst
his wife was pregnant, but there was no help
for it. " As it must be so," he said, " I will go
to Moscow, but during my absence be prudent
and circumspect in your conduct. " Having thus

READMEoops

spoken, he started off on his journey. This happened during Lent. The woman wished to perform her religious duties, and so went to confess. She was a pretty woman. " Why have you such a big belly? " asked the *pope*. — " I have sinned, *batouchka*; I lived with my husband, and became pregnant, and now he has gone to Moscow. " — " To Moscow? " — " Yes, batouchka. " — " Will he stay there long? " — " About a year. " — " Oh, the rascal, he has begun a baby, and has not finished it. That is a deadly sin. There is only one thing for it; I am your spiritual father, and I must finish the child, but for my trouble you must give me three pieces of linen. " — " Do me this kindness, " implored the woman. " Save me from this deadly sin, and finish the baby. But as for that rascal when he returns from Moscow, I will scratch out both his eyes. " — " Well, my dear, I am ready to perform this service for you. The case is urgent; for you will be delivered before your husband's return. " Naturally the *pope* lost no time in performing his promise.

But the priest was married, and even had two daughters, and his great fear was that his wife should hear about the affair. The peasant's wife had been delivered a long time when her husband came back from Moscow. When she saw him enter the *izba* she began to abuse him violently. " Oh, you son of a bitch! You scoundrel! He advised me to be steady and well-behaved, and he himself went away without finishing the baby he had made! It was very fortunate for me that the *batouchka* put the last touch; otherwise I should have been in a pretty fix. " These words left no doubt in the peasant's mind, as to his conjugal mishap. " Patience, " he said to himself, " that long-haired heretic will have to settle accounts with me some day. "

Some time after that, the *pope*, who lived close to the church, was celebrating mass. It was summer time, and the peasant was going to work in his field. He had need of a harrow, and as the *pope* possessed three, the peasant went to him to ask for the loan of one. Being always afraid that the *moujik* would tell his wife about his pranks, the *pope* did not like to refuse him anything. " Take them all three, " he replied. — " But they will not give them to me in your absence, *batouchka*. Call out through the window to the *popadia* to give me all three. " — " Very good, my friend: Go. "

The peasant presented himself to the *pope's* wife, and said. " Madam, the *batouchka* has ordered all three of you to give me your coyntes. " — " You must be out of your mind, friend. " — " Ask him yourself. He has this minute told me so. " The *popadia* cried to her husband. " *Pope*! do you wish us to give the *moujik* —? " — " Yes, yes, give him all three. " There was nothing to be

done but obey, and they did so. The peasant
futtered them one after the other; he began with
the *popadia* and ended with the youngest
daughter; then he returned home. When the
pope came back from the church, his wife loaded
him with abuse. " Oh, devil and heretic! Are
you mad? You have brought dishonor on both
your daughters. Had I been the only one it would
have been bad enough, but you ordered him to
have all three of us. " The *pope* tore his beard,
and rushed off to the *moujik's* house. " You shall
be brought to justice; you have dishonored my
daughters. " — " Don't be angry, *batouchka*, "
replied the peasant, " You like to finish other
people's children, and what is more, accept pieces
of linen as the reward of your trouble. Now we
are quits. " The *pope* was reconciled with the
moujik, and thenceforth they were good friends.

ANOTHER VERSION

In another version of this story it is an uncle
who finishes the child begun by his nephew.
Ivan seeks some method of paying out his uncle
Kouzma. One day the latter is absent from home,
and only the women are left in the house. Vanka
takes a cord, fastens it to the horns of his cow,
and leads the animal through the village. His
aunt sees him through the window. " Certainly, "

she says, "Vanka must be completely ruined; he is going to sell his last cow. Daughter-in-law, go and ask him where he is taking it? " The young woman went into the street; " Where are you taking the cow? " she asked. — " I am angry with my wife, " replied Vanka, " and I will give the cow to any one who will let me futter her . " —" You go with him, daughter-in-law, " said the aunt; " it is not right that the cow should fall into the hands of strangers . " — That was also the daughter-in-law's opinion. " Take the cow into our court, " she cried to Vanka. He took the animal into his aunt's stable and fastened it to a pillar; then he threw the daughter-in-law on the straw, and after having enjoyed her, he wanted to sew up her slit and took a needle and cotton out of his pocket for that purpose. She was frightened, and ran home as quickly as possible.

" Well! Where is the cow?" asked the aunt. " Go yourself. " Replied the daughter-in-law, amid her sobs. " If he had but futtered me, that would have been all right, but not content with that he wanted to sew up my slit. It was too large, he said. " —" Then you go, Matrechka, " the aunt said to her daughter. " If you lose your virtue at least it will not be for nothing, for we shall have the cow. " Matrechka went to Vanka. He laid her on the straw, futtered her, then pulled out of his pocket a small knife. " Oh, the

old she-devil, " he said. " No doubt she sent you
in order to spite me! Your slit is all flayed, and
though you are my cousin I will have no pity
on you. I am going to enlarge your gap with my
knife! " Matrechka was frightened, and ran back

to the *izba* in all haste. " Go yourself, you old
witch, " said the girl, sobbing. " He hurt me very
much, and then wanted to cut me open with his
knife. " " If I should go, " said the aunt, " what
do I risk? I am an old woman. "

When she entered the stable, Vanka threw her
on the straw. Then he grinned, and said, " There

is plenty of snow in my cellar, " after which he struck a match, and pretended to set fire to the straw. The old woman ran away as fast as she was able. Then Vanka took his cow home, and went to meet his uncle. " Good day, *diadiouchka*, " he said, when they met. " Good day! I am much obliged to you for having looked after my household during my absence. " — " Why, you have no hair on your head! " — " How can I help it? God took it from me! " — "If you like, I can make it grow again? I have but to whisper two words in your *chapka*, and the thing is done. " — Vanka then took his uncle's cap, went behind a bush and s..t in the cap; then spread a little grass over the filth, and put the cap on the old man's head. " Be sure, uncle, that you wear it three days and never take it off. "

XLIV

The *pope* and his man.

A *pope*, who was married, and had two daughters, had engaged a man-servant. In the spring, he wished to make a pilgrimage. " Look here, friend, " he said to this man before leaving. " You must by my return have dug up all the kitchen garden, and made the flower-beds. " —" Very good, *batouchka*. " During the absence of his

master, the man did scarcely any work in the garden; at the most he had but turned over a bit of ground here and there with a pick; the greater part of the time he had spent in idling and amusement.

When he returned home, the *pope* went with his wife to visit the kitchen-garden, and found it almost as he had left it. " Friend, don't you know how to dig a garden? " — " No. The fact is I don't know. If I had known I should have done it. " — " Very well friend; you go to the house and ask my daughters for a spade, and I will show you how to dig. " The man went to the parsonage, and said point blank to his master's daughters, " Young ladies, your father orders you both to give me your... " — " What? " " You know what! Your coyntes. " The *pope's* daughters rated him soundly. " There is no cause to abuse me. The *batouchka* wants you to make haste as I must not waste my time here; I have all the garden-beds to dig. If you don't believe me, ask him yourselves. "

One of the two sisters ran out on the steps. " *Batouchka*, " she cried, " did you order me to give that to the man-servant? " " Yes, give it quickly; why are you keeping him? " " Well, sister, " said the girl, as she returned into the room; " there is nothing for it but to obey, since our father has ordered it. " — Then they both lay down, and the man-servant did as he wished.

Then he took a spade that was in the hall, and
ran to the kitchen-garden, where his master was
awaiting him.

After he had shown the man-servant how to
dig up the beds, the *pope* returned to the house,
with his wife, and found both his daughters in
tears. " Why are you weeping? " — " How can
we do otherwise, *batouchka*? You yourself ordered us to be outraged by the man-servant . " —
" What do you mean be outraged? " — " Yes,
you ordered us to give him . . . . " —" Well,
what? I ordered you to give him a spade. " —
" A spade? He has dishonored us both, and
caused us to lose our innocence. "

On hearing these words, the *pope* flew into a
violent rage; he seized a pickaxe, and ran
straight off to the garden. The servant-man
guessed that harm was intended him, when
he saw his master advancing toward him, armed
with a pickaxe, so he dropped his spade and ran
as fast as he could. The *pope* pursued
him, but the man ran the faster, and was soon
out of sight. Wishing to catch the scoundrel, the
priest accosted a peasant he met on the road.
" Good day, friend. " — " Good day, *batouchka*. "
— " Have you met a servant-man on the road? "
— " I don't know; I passed a lad who was
flying like an arrow. " — " That is he! Come
with me, *moujik*, and help me to catch him, and
I will reward you for your trouble. " — " Will-

ingly, *batouchka.* " — They started off together.
A *Tsigane* happened to pass. " Good day, *Tsigane,* " said the *pope.* — " Good day, *batouchka.* "
—" Have you passed a lad on your road? " —
" I saw one, *batouchka,* who passed by me with
the rapidity of lightning. " — " That is the man!
Help us to catch him and I will be grateful to
you " — " Willingly, *batouchka.* " They all
three started off together.

During this time the man-servant had changed
his clothes, and now presented himself to the
pope in a fresh dress. The *pope* did not recognise him, and asked, " Well, friend, did you
meet a *moujik* on your road? " — " Yes, he took
refuge in such and such a village. " — " Come,
friend! help us to find him! " — " Willingly,
batouchka. " All four set off to look for the *pope's*
man-servant. They arrived at a village, after walking all day, but they had not caught him when
night came on. Where were they to sleep? They
came to a house where a widow lived, and asked
her if they might stay there. " Good people, "
replied the widow, " there has been a flood in
my house; and you stand a chance of being
drowned! " But they pleaded so hard, that she
ended by giving them hospitality.

It should be mentioned that the widow's lover
had promised to come and see her that night.
The four men entered the *izba,* and all settled
themselves to sleep the best way they could.

" Suppose there should be a flood? " the *pope*
said to himself. In case such a thing should
occur, he placed a large trough on a table, and
then got in it. " If a flood should happen, "
he thought, " the trough will float on the water. "
— The *Tsigane* lay on the hearth of the stove,
with his head in the ashes; the *moujik* stretched
himself on a bench which was in front of the
table; as to the *pope's* servant, he took his
place on a stool near the window.

As soon as they lay down, all the travellers
closed their eyes. The servant was the only one
who did not sleep. He heard some one approach
the window; then he heard the words, " Open,
my love. " It was the widow's gallant who came
to see her. The servant rose, opened the window,
and said to the visitor; " Ah, my dear, you
arrive very inopportunely. I have strangers lodg-
ing in my house. Come tomorrow night. " —
" All right, my dear; but lean out of the window that I may kiss you at least. " — The servant turned his back to the window and presented his arse to the lover, who covered it with
kisses. " Adieu, dearest, I will come and see
you tomorrow night. Take care of yourself. "
—" Come, my love; but before you leave, dearest, let me take your yard in my hands; that
will be a solace for me. " The lover lugged out
his tool and approached the window. " Here it
is, dear; caress it. " The servant took in his

hand the object which was presented to him, and caressed it several times, then, pulling his knife out of his pocket, he cut the genital parts of the gallant clean off. The lover uttered loud screams, and returned home more dead than alive.

The servant closed the window, sat on the bench, and began to wag his jaws as though he were eating something. The *moujik*, hearing the noise, awoke. " What are you eating, friend? " he asked. — " Oh, I found on the table a piece of sausage, but I cannot manage to eat it; it is not cooked. " — " That doesn't matter, friend; let me taste. " — " There is not too much for me; but never mind, I will give you a bit: enjoy it. " — And he gave the yard he had cut off to the *moujik*. He greedily carried it to his mouth, but try as he might his teeth would make no impression on the supposed sausage. " I give it up, friend, " he said. " It can't be eaten; it is raw meat. " — " Well, put it in the stove, and when it is cooked, you can eat it. " — The *moujik* approached the stove with the sausage, which he put in the *Tsigane's* mouth, and after having left it there a long time, again tried to eat it. — " No, it is impossible! This sausage is too raw; even the fire has no effect on it. " — " Well, that will do, leave it there; if the mistress of the house hears you, she will grumble. The fire must be spread about the stove; pour

some water on it, that our hostess may not see what you have been doing. " — " But where shall I find some water? " — " Oh, piss on it, that is better than going into the court. " The *moujik* followed this advice, and well watered the *Tsigane's* visage. This made the *Tsigane* imagine that a flood was taking place, and he cried with all his might, " Hallo, *batouchka*, we are being drowned. "

His cries awoke the *pope*, who immediately tried to set his improvised cradle afloat, and he and the trough came tumbling to the floor. " Oh, Lord!" groaned the priest, who had broken all his ribs, " when a little child tumbles, Providence puts a cushion under it to break its fall, but when the same accident happens to an old man, the devil brings him a harrow. All my bones are broken. I am sure I shall never find my rascal of a servant. " — " You would do well not to look after him, " remarked the servant. " You had better go home and get your wounds dressed. "

ANOTHER VERSION

A *pope* had hired a man-servant, and said to him one morning: " We will have a bit to eat, and then we will go and thresh the wheat. " They sat at table and ate a rapid breakfast, and the *pope's*

wife then brought three eggs; two for her husband, and one for the servant. The meal being finished, the two men went off to the barn, and each took a flail and began to work. But where the *pope* struck two blows, the servant struck but one. The priest remarked this, and was dissatisfied with the servant. " Is this a joke, friend? I thresh properly, but you only toy with your work. My flail does twice as much work as yours. " —" *Batouchka,* " replied the servant, " at breakfast you ate two eggs and I but one; that is why I have less strength. " " Why did you not say so before, friend? I would have ordered my wife to give you a second egg. Go to the house, and tell her to give you one, and when you have eaten it you can come back. "

The servant threw down his flail, ran to the *izba,* and said to the master's wife: " *Matouchka!* the *pope* orders you to give me.... " — " Give you what? " — " You can guess what: Your person. Only make haste for the *batouchka* ordered me to return at once. " — " Have you lost your senses, cursed rogue? What are you saying? " — " Oh ! Well, ask the *pope* himself if you do not believe me. " — The *popadia* went into the court. " *Batouchka!* " she cried, " do you want me to give that to the man? " — " Haven't you given it yet! " replied the *pope*. "Make haste, do not detain him; he must come back and work. " — The *popadia* returned

into the house. " No; you did not deceive me, "
she said to the servant, and lay down on the
bench in front of the table. The lad performed
lustily; after which, fearing to be surprised by
the *pope*, he made haste away, but in jumping
over the table he left behind him some tell-tale
drops. Of course he did not return to the barn.

The *pope*, however, who was still threshing
the wheat, said to himself, " How is it that the
man does not return? I must go and look after
him. " He then walked into the *izba* and asked
his wife: " Where is the servant ? " — "As
soon as the business was finished, he left. " —
The priest thought that the *popadia* meant the
egg; he approached the table, noticed the liquid
that was spilled thereon, and said to his wife:
" It is evident you gave him a boiled egg, but
he did not eat it properly; he has let some of the
white fall on the table (1). "

The *popadia* looked, and then cried: " The
rascal! When he left me, he jumped over the
table, and then, no doubt, these drops came from
his tool. I must clean up the mess. " — " What?
What? " asked the *pope*. " What did he do to
you? " — " Why he did as you ordered him:

(1) In another version he approaches the table and
says: " Ah, mother, you have eaten an omelette with
the servant, I see, but you have spilled some of the
white. " Thereupon he sprinkles some salt on the supposed white of egg, and licks it up, and thus ends the
tale.

he futtered me. " On hearing this, the *pope* tore
his long hair, and reproached his wife bitterly:
" Oh, cursed whore! " Then he harnessed his
horse and set off in pursuit of the man-
servant.

The latter seeing his master coming, hastily
daubed himself with mud, and when he had
made himself unrecognizable, advanced to meet
the priest. " Good day, *batouchka*! " — " Good
day, friend. " —" Where are you going? " —
" I am looking for my man-servant. " — " Take
me with you. " — " But who are you. " —
" Griaznoff. " — " Be it so; we will journey
together. " The two set off, and on the road
they met a *Tsigane*, who also asked permission
to join them. The three travelled together. They
had arrived near a river when night fell. On the
river bank was a little house, in which lived a
widow whom her lover came to see at night.
They begged her to let them lodge in her house.
At first she refused. " It is quite impossible! Tonight my house will be flooded, and you will all
be drowned in your sleep. " —" Oh no! we shall
find means to escape the flood. " Finally the widow
gave way, and consented to receive the travellers
in her house.

The *pope* installed himself in the shed: " Here, "
he thought, " I shall surely be in safety. The
water will not reach to this height. " The *Tsigane*
hooked a trough to the ceiling and lay down

therein after having provided himself with a knife. " If the inundation should take place, " he thought, " I will cut the cords which support the trough, and it will float on the water. " The woman of the house slept on the stove. The man-servant suspected that she had a lover, and placed himself near the window. " If I am drowned, so much the worse, " he said, "one can but die once. " During the night he heard some one approach the window. " Who goes there? " — " It is I, " replied the lover. — " Well, have you brought anything? " — " I have brought half a bottle of brandy, and some chitterlings. " — " Very good; give them here. " The other obeyed. Then the servant said: " I cannot receive you this evening, for I have travellers staying here, but let me at least hold your tool in my hands for a minute, and that will console me. The lover exhibited his member; the servant laid hold of it roughly and then looked round to see he could not find a stick wherewith to baste the visitor's ribs; by chance his hand fell on a knife with which he cut the yard of the lover clean off, who return-ed home in a most lamentable condition.

The servant at once set to work to empty the bottle and eat the chitterlings, but *popes* have keen noses for such things! The *batouchka* awoke " Griaznoff, " he cried, " what are you eating? " — " Chitterlings. " — " Give me one." — The servant gave him the gallant's tool that he had cut off. The *pope* tried in vain to bite it, and was obliged to return it to the servant. " It is too hard, " he remarked. " It has never been cooked. "

Then they all went to sleep again, but the servant thought of another trick. He climbed up to the loft, and began to piss on the *pope's* face. " The water is rising. We shall be drowned, " cried the priest, and fell heavily to the floor. On hearing this, the *Tsigane* cut the cords which held the trough in which he was lying, and he too fell with a bang to the ground. They picked themselves up, both more or less bruised, and made off as fast as they were able. As to the man-servant he now lives with the widow (1).

(1) In yet another version a cobbler is travelling alone; a tailor meets him, and says: " Good day ! A good journey to you. " " Good day. " — " May I accompany you? " — " So be it! come with me. " They journey together and meet a German, who says, " Good day! A good journey to you, friends. Will you accept me as a companion? " — " Can you be our companion? We are Russians and you are a German. " — " Let me come with you, friends. " — " Very well: come. " (The remainder of the story differs little from that just given.) The travellers stop at a widow's house to pass the night, notwithstanding the objections raised by the mistress of the house. The cobbler lies near the window, the tailor on a bench near the stove, and the German in a trough which he has previously fastened to the ceiling. The widow's lover arrives. " Dearest, " he says, " at least let me kiss you. " The cobbler presents his arse, and the lover kisses it. " What large chops you have, " he remarks. Then the cobbler pisses in the German's mouth, and makes him tumble to the ground (as in the previous version). " The German is a sly fox, " says the cobbler, " but we have caught him all the same. "

XLV

The *pope's* family, and the
man-servant.

In our country there lived a *pope* who had a
wife, three daughters, and a man-servant. The
latter wanted to obtain the favors of his master's
daughters, but he did not dare to speak boldly.
There came a feast day; the servant took a saucepan and carried it to the coach-house, then he put
some water in the saucepan, lighted a fire, and
began to boil the water. When the *pope* returned
from saying mass, he sat at table with his wife and
daughters, and asked, "Where is the man? " — " He
has been working in the coach-house ever since
the morning, " replied the *popadia*. " What !
impious wretch! you set him to work today? A day
like this? Have you not the fear of God before
your eyes? " — " We did not send him, he went
himself. " " Go and fetch him, " said the *pope*
to his eldest daughter; " tell him to come to
dinner. "

The young woman ran to the coach-house.
" What are you cooking there? " she asked. —
" Something good. " — " Let me taste! " —
" Let me futter you! " — The *pope's* daughter
tucked up her clothes and the lad futtered her,

after which he gave her some of his stew. " —Why, it is water!" she said, and ran away. The *pope*, when he saw her return to the *izba*, said: " Why does not the man come? " — " He is at work. " — " Fool! you ought to have told him to leave off and come to dinner. *You* go and fetch him, " he added addressing his second daughter, " and bring him here. " The young girl went at once to the coach-house, and put the same question as her sister had done: " What are you cooking, gardener? " — " Something good! " — " Let me taste. " — " Let me futter you! " She consented, and when the lad had futtered her, he let her taste his stew. " Why, it is water! " she said, and returned in haste to the house. " Well! where is the man? " asked the father. — " He won't come, he is still busy. " The *pope* sent his youngest daughter to the coach-house, and she in her turn, asked, " What are you cooking? " — " Something good! " — " Let me taste. " — " Let me roger you, just once. " — The young girl was as willing as her sisters, and in return the man let her drink some of the water out of his saucepan, after which she returned to the *izba*. " You are all fools, " said the *pope* angrily, " you go wife, and tell the man to come at once. "

The *popadia* then went to the coach-house. " What are you messing with there? " she began. — " Something delicious. " — " Let me taste a mouthful. " " If you will allow me to grind you. "

The *popadia* at first refused, but the man was obstinate, and as she had a great desire to know what he was cooking, she let herself be futtered to obtain the favor of tasting a little water. " Well, *matouchka*, " then asked the servant, " is my stew good? " —He emptied the saucepan

and went in to dinner. " Why did you not come before, you fool? " said the *pope*; " it is a sin to work today. " —All sat down to table, and a pie was served: the *pope* cut it up and distributed a slice to each guest. The *popadia* offered hers to the servant: " Here, " she said. " I will give you my share for what you did just now! " The girls hastened to imitate their mother and " Here, gardener, " said all three, handing him their slices of pie. " That is for what you did just now. " The *pope* seeing this, did the same: " Here, take my share, for what you did just now. " —" What! did he futter you too! " the *popadia* asked her husband. —" And you, has he futtered you? " — " I should think so, rather, " replied all four women together. The *pope* then flew into a violent rage, and turned the servant out of doors.

XLVI

The comb.

A *pope* had a daughter who was still innocent. When the spring came, he saw about having his hay cut, but he arranged with each of his workmen that he should not pay him if his daughter could leap over the hay he had cut. Many of them accepted these conditions, and were obliged to return home without touching any wages for their work; for as soon as they had mown a good-sized heap of hay, the *pope's* daughter came and jumped over it.

At last a bold lad presented himself, and offered to cut the priest's hay; he was told the conditions, accepted them, and began to work. When he had cut a certain quantity of hay, he made a heap of it, and lay down beside it; then he pulled out his yard, and made it stand. Just then the *pope's* daughter came to see how he was working, and finding him thus engaged, asked; " What are you doing, *moujik*? " — " Seeing to my comb. " — " What do you comb with that? " — " If you like, I will comb you; lie down on the hay. " — The girl did so, and the man combed her in a way that can be guessed. — " What a good comb! " said the *popovna* when she got up. Then she tried to jump over the hay, but only succeeded in soiling her linen.

She went to her father, and said, " The heap is too big, I cannot jump over it. " — " Ah! daughter, then surely we have found an excellent man. I will engage him for a year. " — When the *moujik* demanded his wages, the *pope* would not consent to let him go. " I wish to keep you for a year, my friend. " — " Very good, *batouchka.* "

The laborer, therefore, remained in the *pope's* house, to the great satisfaction of the *popovna*, who came to him at night, and said, " Comb me a little! " — " No, I will not comb you for nothing; give me a hundred rubles, and then you can buy the comb. " — The young girl went, and fetched a hundred rubles, and gave them to the man, who after that, combed her every night.

But some time afterwards, the *moujik* had a quarrel with the *pope*, and he asked for his money, and left. The *popovna* was not at home at the time. When she returned to the house, she asked where the man was. " He has left. "

replied the *pope*. " I paid him what I owed him and he went away. " — " Oh, father, what have you done? He has taken my comb with him. " Thereupon the girl started in pursuit of the young man, and overtook him on the banks of a little brook. He had tucked up his trousers, and was preparing to ford the brook. " Give me my comb! " cried the *popovna*. The *moujik* picked up a stone, and threw it into the water. " Take it, " he cried, after which he crossed to the other side of the brook, and ran away as fast as he could. The young girl tucked up her skirts, entered the water, and began to search for the comb, but though she groped all over the bed of the brook, it was lost labor.

Presently there chanced to pass, a *barine* in his carriage. " What are you looking for, my dear? " he asked. —" A comb; I bought it for a hundred rubles from our man-servant, but, when he left our house, he took it away with him. I started off after him, and when I caught him, he threw it into the water. " The *barine* got out of his carriage, took off his trousers, and entered the water to search for the girl's comb. All at once his tool caught the girl's eye, she seized it with both hands, and cried: " Ah, there is my comb! Give it to me! " — " What are you doing, you shameless wretch! " cried the other. " Let me go. " —" No, it is you who are shameless! You want to take what doesn't belong to you. Give me my comb. " And still holding the *barine* by the tool, the *popovna* led him back to her father's house.

The *pope* was at the window, and saw his daughter arrive holding the *barine* by the most tender part of his body, whilst she cried, " Give me back my comb, rascal. " — " *Batouchka!* save me from a death I have not deserved, and I will never forget you, " said the poor man, supplicatingly. What was to be done? The priest quickly pulled his yard out of his trousers, showed it at the window to his daughter, and cried: " Daughter! Daughter! Here is your comb! "

" Yes, that is mine really, " she cried. " Yes, it is red at the tip. And I was stupid enough to think the *barine* had taken it! " With that she let go her victim, and rushed into the house. The *barine* made off as fast as he could.

As soon as she was in the house, the *pope's* daughter asked; " Papa, where is my comb? " —Her father scolded her soundly. " Oh, you good-for-nothing! " And then he cried to his wife: " Look *matouchka!* she has lost her honor. " " Enough, *batouchka,* " replied the wife to her husband, " look into the matter yourself, and put it in order. " The *pope* instantly took off his trousers and futtered his daughter. When he was at the height of the enjoyment, he whinnied, and cried, " No, no! Our daughter has not lost her

honor. " —" *Batouchka*! " said the *popadia*,
" pick up her honor again. " —" Be easy, *matou-chka*, it will not fall out, I have driven it well
in. But our daughter is still young: she does not
know how to lift up her legs properly. " —
" Lift them higher, my child! Higher! " said the
mother. " Ah, *matouchka*, " — replied the *pope*,
" She is still all in a heap. " Thus did the
popovna find her comb again, and henceforth the
pope slept with both his wife and his daughter.

XLVII

Making it warm.

A *moujik* had three sons, the two eldest were intelligent, but the youngest was a fool. " My dear children, " said the father; " how will you support me, now that I am old? " " By our labor, " said the two eldest, but the youngest — like the fool that he was — replied: " By what could I support you better than by my tool? "

The next day, the eldest son shouldered his scythe, and started off to find some hay to cut. On the road, he met the *pope*, who asked him where he was going. " I am looking for work. " he replied. " I want to hire myself out to cut hay. " —" Come home with me, " replied the *pope*, " but there are conditions. I will give you a hundred rubles if my daughter cannot jump over the hay you can cut in the day, but if she can, you will not have a kopeck. " —" There's no danger of her jumping over it, " thought the lad, and he accepted the proposed arrange-ment.

The *pope* led him to the field, and said, " This is the place, my man, begin and mow. " The young man set to work immediately, and when evening came, he had mown a heap of quite enormous size. But the *pope's* daughter came and jumped over it, and the young man returned home quite despondent.

The same luck happened to the second brother.

" Very well, " said then the youngest, " I must go and find some work for my prickle. " He took his scythe, and set off, and also met the *pope*, who engaged him on the same conditions as his elder brothers. The fool began to mow but when he had cut one or two swathes along the field, he took off his trousers and lay down, with his backside in the air.

The *pope's* eldest daughter came. " Why are you not mowing, my lad? " she asked. — " One minute! just let me get some heat in my arse so that I shall not be cold in the winter. " — " Warm mine for me too, please. In the winter we travel a good deal, and are always shivering with cold. " — " Turn your backside, then, and I will put some warmth into it." The girl put herself in the proper position and the fool brandished his flapper and put some warmth into the *popovna*'s slit, until she sweated great drops. " There, that is enough, " he said at last; " now you have enough to last you all the winter. " She ran home. " Ah, my dears, " she cried to her sisters, " the man-servant has well warmed my arse for me. He and I are both dripping with sweat. " The two younger sisters hastened in their turn to the man-servant, and were supplied with warmth for the winter; but as far as mowing the field was concerned he hardly did any work at all.

The *pope* came with his eldest daughter, and seeing how little hay had been cut, said in a tone of assurance: " My man, you had better return home. My daughter will have no trouble in jumping over that little bit. " — " That remains to be seen. " The *pope* ordered his daughter to jump, but the moment she lifted up her dress to obey her father's commands, a stream of liquid ran all down her leg. " You see, " observed the young man, " that you spoke too hastily. "

The *pope* was vexed and sent for his two other daughters. " If none of the three can jump over the hay, " he said to the young man, " I will give you a hundred rubles for each of them. " — " Very good. " But it happened to the two younger daughters as it had happened to the elder. After having received three hundred rubles from the *pope,* the fool returned home. " Look here, " he said to his family, " What I have gained with my prickle! See how much money it has brought in! "

XLVIII

The burial of the dog (and the goat).

A certain *moujik* had a dog. Being annoyed
with the animal, he took it into a wood, and fastened it to an oak-tree. The dog began to scratch
with its paws, till at last the tree was so under-
mined that it was blown down by the wind. The
next day, the peasant went to the wood; the idea
came to him that he would like to look at the
dog. He went to the place where the dog was
tied, and what did he see? The tree thrown
down, and in the hole made by the torn-up roots
was a large pot full of gold.

The peasant, delighted at this windfall, returned home as quickly as he could, and came
back again with a cart, in which he placed the
treasure and also the dog. When he arrived
home, he said to the women of his household:
" Listen! I expect that henceforth you will treat
my dog with the greatest respect. If you do not
take care of him, or if you let him want food,
you will get into trouble with me. "

In obedience to this order, the women paid
every attention to the dog, they bestowed upon it
the most delicious food, they made it a soft bed
and petted it in all sorts of ways. As to the master

of the house he trusted no one but the dog: Whenever he had to leave home, he hung his keys round the dog's neck.

But after some time, the animal fell ill, and died. The peasant determined to pay it funeral honors. He took five-thousand rubles, and went to the *pope*. " *Batouchka*, my dog is dead, and he has left you a legacy of five-thousand rubles, on condition that you give him Christian burial. " " Very good, my friend! I am not allowed to bring him into the church, but I can bury him all the same. Do you get all ready, and I will come tomorrow and see the corpse removed. "

The *moujik* made a coffin and placed the carcass of the dog therein; the next morning there came the *pope*, accompanied by the deacon and the choir, all clad in their church robes. They performed the burial service, and carried the dog to the cemetery and placed it in a grave. The *pope* was obliged to give part of the money he had received to his assistants, but he distributed it in so niggardly a fashion that the choristers, out of spite, informed the bishop that Christian burial had been given to a dog.

The prelate summoned the *pope* to appear before him. " How it is you have dared, " he said, " to bury a wretched cur? " and he put the *pope* in prison. Then the peasant took ten-thousand rubles, and went to the bishop to obtain the *pope's* release. " What is your want? " asked the bishop. " My dog is dead, " replied the *moujik*, " and he bequeathed ten-thousand rubles to your Holiness, and five-thousand to the *pope*. " —" Yes, my son, I had heard of it, and if I put the *pope* in prison, it was because the impious wretch did not carry the dog's body to the church. He ought to have said a mass for him. " The prelate took the ten-thousand rubles bequeathed to him by the dog, and not content with merely setting the *pope* at liberty, named him archdeacon; as to the choristers, he had them incorporated in the militia.

ANOTHER VERSION

An old man lived alone with his wife; they had no children and no animals except a he-goat. The old man followed no trade; he made a few bark shoes, and that was his only means of existence. The goat was used to his master's ways, and followed him whenever he went out. One day, the old man went to the wood to seek for bark, and the goat followed him. They came to the wood, and the old peasant began to tear off the bark of the lime-trees; meanwhile the goat browsed here and there. Suddenly its fore-feet sunk in some loose earth, it commenced to struggle, and in so doing unearthed a pot full of gold.

Seeing the goat scratching the ground, the old man approached, and perceived the treasure. Filled with unspeakable joy, he threw away the bark, took the precious pot, and conveyed it home. " See, old man, " said his wife to him, when she had heard about the find. " God has sent us this fortune in our old age, as a recompense for the poverty we have suffered so many years. Now we can enjoy a time of ease. " — " No, old woman, " replied her husband. " This money was found, not by us, but by the goat; consequently, we should take great care of him, and look after his welfare before thinking of our own. "

From that time, the old man and his wife applied themselves to making the goat comfortable, but they also lived well; the old man forgot how to dress bark; in short, from that day, they lived in ease, and free from every care. Some time afterwards the goat died. The husband consulted with his wife, as to what ought to be done under the circumstances. " If, " he said, " we should throw the goat to the dogs we should be guilty of sin in the eyes of God and men, for it is to him we owe our happiness. It would be better to go to the *pope*, and beg him to give the goat Christian burial, as they do to other corpses. "

Thereupon, the old man went off to the *pope*. " Good day, *batouchka* " he began, and making a low bow. — " Good day, my friend! What

news? " — " Oh, *batouchka*, I have come to ask
a favor of your Holiness. My goat is dead, and
I wish to ask you to bury it. " — On hearing
this, the *pope* flew into a violent rage, he seized
the old man by the beard, and shook him violently. " Oh, cursed wretch, what are you thinking
of? Bury a stinking goat! " —" But, *batouchka*,
the goat was quite orthodox. He has left you
two-hundred rubles. " — " Listen, you old
grey-beard, " replied the priest. " If I smite you,
it is not because you ask me to bury your goat,
but because you have deferred informing me of
his death until this moment. Perhaps he has
already been dead a long time. " And after
he had pocketed the peasant's two-hundred
rubles, the *pope* continued: " Now go at once
and find the elder deacon; tell him to prepare
everything, and we will come at once and bury
the goat. "

The old man went to the deacon and said: " Be
good enough, father deacon, to come to my house
to prepare a funeral. " —" Who then is dead
at your house? " — " Why, you know my old
goat, it is he who is dead. " " What! " said the
deacon, and he gave his visitor a good buffet on
the head. — " Do not beat me, father deacon, "
replied the peasant, " my goat was quite orthodox, and when he died he left you a hundred
rubles for performing the funeral. " — " Oh,
what a fool you are, although you are so old, "

said the deacon. " Why did you not tell me before that he died a good Christian? Go quickly to the sexton, and tell him to toll the bell for the goat's funeral. "

The old man went to the sexton. " Go and ring, " he said, "for the death of my goat. " The sexton was angry, and gripping the old man's beard, shook him violently. " Leave go, please, " cried the visitor. " My goat was orthodox. He left you fifty rubles for his funeral. "
—" Why did you not say so before? If I had only known that I should long ago have tolled the bell for him. " Having thus spoken, the sexton hurried off to the church and tolled the bell lustily.

The *pope* and the deacon came and performed the burial service at the old man's house; after which they put the goat in a coffin and went and buried it in the cemetery. However, the affair was bruited about the parish, and the bishop at last heard that Christian burial had been given to a goat. The *pope* and the peasant were summoned to appear before the bishop. "What! " he said to them; " Have you dared to bury a goat? Impious wretches that you are! " — " But this goat was not at all like others, " remarked the old man. " Before he died, he bequeathed a thousand rubles to your Grace. " — " Why, you old fool, what I am reproaching you with is not the fact that you had him buried, but that you allowed him to die without the sacraments. " The bishop took the thousand rubles, and sent away the two accused persons acquitted of the charge brought against them.

XLIX

The sentence concerning the cows.

In a village there lived a *pope* and a *moujik;* the former possessed seven cows, the latter had but one, and even that was lame. But a *pope* is naturally covetous, and this one sought some means by which he could appropriate the *moujik's* only cow. " That will make eight, " he said to himself.

One day when it was a festival, and all the peasants had come to the church, the *pope* left the altar, and pretending to read from a book that was open before him, pronounced these words in a loud voice: " Listen, my brothers! If any one will give a cow to his spiritual pastor, God will reward him according to his infinite goodness, and this single cow will bring him seven others! "

Our *moujik*, who was amongst the worshippers, said to himself on hearing these words, " Of what use is our single cow? She does not give enough milk for all the family. I will do as it says in the Scriptures, and offer my cow to the *pope*. Perhaps God will reward me for it. " As soon as the mass was over, the *moujik* returned home, put a cord around the cow's horns, and led her to the priest's house. " Good day, *batouchka*, " he said on entering. — " Good day, friend! Have you any good news to tell? " — " I was at church today, and I heard that it says in the Scriptures: If any one gives a cow to his spiritual father it will bring him seven others. Very well, *batouchka*! I come to offer my cow to your Holiness. " —" Quite right, friend; I see that you listen to the holy word. God will reward you sevenfold. Take your cow to the cow-house, friend, and put it along with mine. "

The peasant complied, but when he returned home, his wife reproached him bitterly. " Why, you rascal, have you given the brown cow to the *pope?* I suppose you want us to die of hunger like dogs? " —" What a fool you are, " replied her husband. " Did you not hear what the *pope* said at the church? Wait a bit, and our cow will be restored with seven others, and then you can have as much milk as you like. "

The peasant remained all the winter without a cow. When the spring came, the cows were sent to pasture in the fields, the *pope's* cows being amongst the number. At night-fall the cow-herd drove the cows back to the village, and they went to their proper and respective cow-houses; but the one that the *moujik* had given to the *pope* returned, by force of habit, to its old master's house, and the priest's seven cows were so used to their new companion that they followed it into the peasant's courtyard. The *moujik* was looking out of the window, and said to his wife: " Just look: our cow has brought back seven others. What the *pope* predicted has happened; the word of God is always true. Do you still reproach me with what I did? Now we shall want neither milk nor food. " And he quickly ran into the yard, drove the cows into his cow-house and locked the door.

The *pope*, however, finding that his cows did not come home at night, began to search for them all through the village. He came at last to the peasant and said: " How is it, my friend, that you have taken in cows that do not belong to you? " — " What are you talking about? There are no cows here that do not belong to me; they are mine, for God has given them to me. It was my little brown cow which brought me seven others, in accordance with what you yourself read out in the church, *batouchka*, the other day. " — " You are joking, you son of a dog, they are my cows. " — " No, they are mine! " — The discussion grew warm, and the *pope* finished by saying to the peasant: " May the devil take you! Keep your old cow, but at least give me mine. " — " Would you like a dog's tool ? (1) "

The *pope*, in despair, went and lodged a complaint against the *moujik*. The case was tried in the bishop's court, and the bishop did not know how to decide it, for he had received a bribe of money from the *pope*, and a piece of cloth from the peasant. " I find it very difficult, " he said, " to decide between you, but I have hit upon a plan. You are both to return home, and the one who first arrives here tomorrow shall have the cows. "

The *pope* returned home and said to his wife, " Be careful to call me very early tomorrow morning."

But the *moujik* was not a fool, instead of returning home, he went and hid under the bishop's bed. " I will pass the night here," he said

(1) Equivalent seemingly to: " Don't you wish you may get it? "

to himself. " I shall not sleep, and tomorrow morning I shall be on the spot, and by that means I shall do the *pope* out of the cows. "

Whilst the *moujik* was lying under the bed, he heard some one knock at the door. The bishop rose, went to the door, and asked, " Who is there ? " — " It is I, — the mother abbess — father. "—" Come in, mother abbess, and lie upon the bed."She obeyed. The prelate then began to play with her titties. "What are these?" he asked. " Holy father, they are the mountains of Sion, and below are the valleys. " —The bishop then put his hand on her navel. " And this: — what is this? " —" That is the navel of the earth. " —The Bishop's hand descended still lower, and closed on the coynte of the abbess. " And this: what is this? " —" That, father, is a little hell. " —

"And I, mother, have a sinner, who must be put into hell. " — The act followed the word — that is to say the bishop futtered the mother

abbess, after which he led her out of the room.

Whilst he was absent, the *moujik* slipped away noiselessly, and returned home. The next day the *pope* rose before dawn, and without even stopping to wash, ran with all speed to the bishop's palace. As to the *moujik*, he slept well, idled away the morning, and the sun had long risen when he got out of bed. He breakfasted, and then leisurely made his way to the bishop's palace, where he had been long awaited. " Well, my friend, " said the *pope*, with a mocking smile, " I suppose you stopped at home to cuddle your wife? " The Bishop, addressing the peasant, said: " There can be no doubt that you are the second. " — " Oh, no, your Holiness, the *pope* arrived after me. You have perhaps forgotten that I arrived at your house when you were walking about on the mountains of Sion, and putting a sinner in hell. " The bishop held up both hands, to stop the peasant from saying more. " The cows are yours, *moujik*," he declared, " in fact, it is evident you must have been here first. " Thus the *pope* lost all his cattle, and the *moujik* in the future lived in ease (1).

(1) In another version of the story, the *pope*, when he returns home, sends for his man-servant, to whom he had promised a hundred rubles a year, of which sum he had not paid a stiver in seven years. The man demands his money, and the *pope* replies: " All the seven years you have been with me, you have never confessed. Confess all your sins, and then I will pay you your wages. " The *pope* then asks him if he has ever helped to steal anyone's cattle. " No, *batouchka;* I am not guilty of that, but as I am confessing, I will own that during seven years I have ridden your daughter-in-law. " — " That is not the question, have you ever stolen any cattle? " — " No, *batouchka*, but I have seduced your wife. " — " This is not a time for stupid jokes; did you take away my cows? " — " No, *batouchka*, that sin is not on my conscience; but I will own that my yard has even risen against you. " " Then as you won't confess, remain damned. " The *pope* then paid him and sent him away, and remained without a man-servant and without his cows.

L

The greedy *pope*.

A certain *pope* possessed a rich living, but he was so avaricious that during Lent, he demanded at least a *grivennik* (1) of every worshipper who came to confess; those who did not bring that sum he would not confess, and insulted and abused them into the bargain. " What! you dull beast! You cannot in all the year put aside a *grivennik* for your spiritual father? And must I pray to God for cursed scoundrels like you? "

One day a soldier came to confess to this *pope*, and on the edge of the confessional, he placed a copper *piatak* (2). On seeing this, the priest flew into a violent rage.

"Oh, cursed wretch, " he cried, " what devil put it into your head to offer your spiritual father a copper *piatak*? I suppose it is a joke. " —" How do you expect I can offer you any more, *batouchka*? I give all I can. " — " You can always find money for whores and drink, I suppose; but you think it enough to bring your sins to your spiritual father. In such circumstances you ought to steal something and sell it; then bring the priest

(1) Ten kopecks or about four pence.
(2) Five kopecks or two pence.

the required sum, confess the theft along with
the other sins, and the priest would absolve them
all at the same time. " With that he sent away the
soldier unshriven. " And don't you dare to come
to me again till you have a *grivennick*, " he
said.

" How can I satisfy this *pope*? " thought the
soldier when he was driven out of the confessional.
Casting his eyes round, he saw, near the choir a
priest's staff with a beaver cap on the top of it.
" Let me try to sneak that cap, " he said to himself. He took the cap, slipped noiselessly out of
the church, and went to the inn. There the soldier
sold the cap for twenty rubles, stuffed the
money in his pocket, and putting on one side a
grivennik for the *pope*, returned to the church,
and approached the confessional. " Well, have
you brought me a *grivennik*? " asked the priest.
" Yes, *batouchka*. " —" And how did you obtain
it my son? " — " I am a sinner, *batouchka*. I stole
a fur cap that I sold for a *grivennick*. " " No
matter, " said the priest to the penitent. " God
pardons you, and I absolve you. "

The soldier then left, and the *pope* having
finished confessing his parishioners celebrated
vespers. At the conclusion of the service, he prepared to return home, and went to the spot where
he had left his cap, but no cap could he find, and
he was compelled to return home bare-headed.
His first care on arriving at home was to send

for the soldier. " Now, my son, tell me the truth: have you stolen my cap? " —" I do not know whether it was yours, *batouchka*, but caps of that sort are only worn by *popes* " — " And where did you get it? " — " I found it in your church, on the top of a *pope's* staff, near the choir. " — " Oh, you son of a dog, how dared you steal the cap of your spiritual father? " — " But you yourself, *batouchka*, have absolved me from that sin. "

LI

Laughter and tears.

In a certain country there lived a *pope* who, as he resided on the bank of a river, ferried travellers across the stream. One day, a *bourlak* (1) came down to the ferry. " Hallo! *Batouchka!* ferry me across, " he cried to the *pope*, who was just then on the other side of the river, " Can you pay for the ferry, my son? "

" I would pay you if I had any money, but I have none. " — " Then I won't ferry you across. " — " If you will ferry me over, *batouchka*, I will show you laughter and tears. "

The *pope* thought it over. " What can the man mean by that? " he said to himself, and in short he was so anxious to be shown laughter and tears, that he rowed across, took the *bourlak* on board and ferried him over the river. " Very good, *batouchka!* Turn your boat bottom upwards. " The *pope* turned the boat over — curious to see what was going to happen. The *bourlak* pulled out of his trousers a huge, lusty member, and with it bestowed such a terrific blow on the bottom of the boat that the timbers were stove in and broken. At the sight of such a

(1) A man employed in towing on the Volga.

splendid instrument, the pope at first began to laugh; but then, when he thought of the destruction of his boat, he felt so sad that the tears came to his eyes. " Well, *batouchka*, have I kept my word? " asked the *bourlak*. — " May the devil take you! Go away! " the *bourlak* said farewell, and went on his way.

The priest returned home. As he entered the door he thought of the *bourlak's* member, and that made him laugh, but when he remembered the fate of his boat, he burst into tears. " What is the matter, *batouchka*? " asked his wife. — " You don't know what a misfortune has happened, *matouchka*, " and he told her simply what had occurred. As soon as she heard of her husband meeting with the *bourlak*, the *popadia*, began to reproach him. " Oh, old devil that you are! Why did you let him go? Why did you not bring him back to the house? That was not a *bourlak*, that was my brother! My parents have certainly sent him to pay us a visit and you did not guess it. — Quickly harness the horse, and go after him, or otherwise the poor man will wander about aimlessly, and perhaps even have to return home without having seen us. Oh, my dear brother, if I could only see him for a moment, and ask for some news about my parents. "

The *pope* harnessed his horse, and started off to seek for the *bourlak*, and when he overtook him, said. " Look here, my good man! Why did you conceal from me that you were my wife's brother? When I told her of your exploit, she recognised you at once, and sent me after you to bring you home. " The *bourlak* immediately guessed the riddle. " Yes, " he replied, " that is the truth. I am your wife's brother, but as for you, *batouchka*, I never saw you before, and consequently could not recognise you. " The *pope* took him by the arm, and made him get into the cart. " Sit down, dear boy, sit down! Come along home! My wife and I, thank God, live in ease and happiness, and we have the means to make you comfortable ."

When the cart arrived at the house, the *popadia* ran out to meet the *bourlak*, threw herself on his neck and embraced him. " Oh, my dear brother, what a long time it is since I saw you. And how are they all at home? " —" Much as usual, sister! Our parents sent me to see how you were going on. " —" Why, as for us, brother, up to now, God has been indulgent to our sins, and permitted us to live. " She invited him to sit at the table, offered him various dishes, and an omelette, and brandy. " Eat, dear brother, " she kept repeating every minute. All were merry, and the meal was prolonged till night came.

When it began to get dark, the *popadia* made a bed, and said to her husband. " I am going to sleep here with my brother. We shall talk about our relatives, the living and the dead. As for you, *batouchka*, you will sleep alone upon the stove bench, or in the shed. When all had gone to bed, the *bourlak* attacked the *popadia* so vigorously that she could not help giving a loud cry, which rang through the house. The *pope* heard it, and asked, " What is the matter? " — " Oh, *batouchka*, you don't know what a misfortune has happened. My father is dead. " —" Well, may God have his soul, " said the *pope*, and crossed himself. But soon the *popadia* gave another cry more piercing than the first, and her husband demanded an explanation. " Why are you crying again? " " Oh, *batouchka*, my mother is also dead! " — " May God give her peace. May she repose with the saints. " And this continued all night.

The next morning, the *bourlak* prepared to return home, but the *popadia* would not let him set out fasting, and offered him pie and brandy, and was very attentive. " Whenever you pass in our neighborhood, dear brother; do not forget to call upon us. " The priest added his entreaties to those of his wife. " Call upon us when you like; we shall always be glad to see you. "

The *bourlak* said adieu to his hosts. The *popadia* wished to take her pretended brother a part of the road, and the *Pope* also insisted on accompanying the traveller. They all three started off, and a brisk conversation was maintained on the road. When they were far out in the country, the *popadia* said to her husband: " Return home, *ba-touchka*; there is no need for you to go any farther. I will go alone with my brother a little way."

The priest turned back, but after he had gone some thirty paces, he stopped and turned round to see where they were. In the meantime, the *bourlak*, wishing to give his supposed sister a farewell worthy of him, had laid her down upon the bank by the side of the road, and had set to work to futter her, but in order to deceive the husband, he put his cap on the *popadia's* right foot, and ordered her to lift her leg in the air. Whilst they were taking their pleasure, the foot with the cap on it did not cease to shake; seeing which, the pope said to himself, " What an affectionate relative? He is already a long way off, and nevertheless continues to wave adieux with his cap. " The *pope* also took off his *chapka*, waved it in the air, and cried, " Adieu, brother-in-law; adieu. "

After having received a final and warm farewell from the *bourlak*, the *popadia*, looking radiant with happiness, rejoined her husband. In her joy she began to sing songs. " During all the years I have lived with you, " remarked the *pope*, " this is the first time I ever heard you sing. " — " The reason is, *batouchka*, " she replied, " that I was so glad to see my dear brother. I wonder whether I shall ever see him again? " —" God is very merciful; and perhaps, you will again have that happiness (1). "

LII

The marvelous ointment.

In a certain country there lived a young peasant whose affairs were far from prosperous; a plague had carried off all his horned cattle, and all his horses, except one mare. This animal he pampered in every way, and loved as the apple of his eye; he would have deprived himself of everything in order that his mare should want for nothing. One day, after he had groomed the horse, he began to caress it, and speak tenderly to it: " Oh, my dove! *Matouchka!* There is no one so pretty as you. "

A big peasant-girl, the daughter of a neighbor, heard these words, and when the girls of the village met in the street, she said to them; " My dears, whilst I was in our garden, Gregori, our neighbor, was grooming his mare, then he made love to it, embraced it, and made soft speeches to it, like, 'My dove! *Matouchka!* There is no one so pretty as you in all the world.' "

(1) In a variation of this story the *pope* discovers how he has been deceived, but deems it advisable not to say anything to the *bourlak*, for remembering how the boat was smashed—he thinks to himself, " If he were to strike me with his tool, he would kill me. "

From that time, the young man was a butt for all the jests of the village girls; whenever they met him, they cried, "Oh, *matouchka!* My dove! " The poor young man did not dare to show himself, and fell into a profound grief. His old aunt perceived it. " Why, are you so sad, Gricha? Why do you hang your head? "

He told her the whole affair. " That is nothing Gricha, " she replied. " I will manage that. Come tomorrow to my house. Be easy; they shall not tease you any more. "

The old woman practised medicine, which made her an important personage in the locality, and the young girls often used to visit her in the evening. That evening she had a visit from the peasant girl who had set about the rumor that Gregori was in love with his mare. " My daughter, " said the old woman to her, " come and see me tomorrow morning, I have something to tell you. " —" Very good, granny. "

The next morning, the young man got up, dressed himself, and went to his aunt's house. " Now, Gricha, be ready to act at the right moment; but at present get behind the stove, and remain quite quiet until I call you. " — Hardly had taken his place behind the stove than the peasant girl arrived. " Good day, granny. " — " Good day, my dove! This is what I have to tell you. You are in a very bad way. You are very ill, my dear. " — " I? granny! I think I am quite well. " —" No, my dove! You have an internal complaint that it frightens me even to think of. At present you don't feel anything, but when it reaches your heart there will be no hope for you, and you will die. Let me feel your belly. " — " Feel, granny, " replied the young girl; and she almost began to cry, she was so frightened. — " There! you see I was not mistaken, " said the old woman, after she had felt the abdomen. " Yesterday, at the first glance, I guessed that you had something serious the matter. It is a jaundice of the heart. " — " Cure me, I beg of you, granny. " — " Of course as you are ill I must try to cure you; but can you bear the treatment? I warn you that it will be painful. " — " Do what you like to me. If you cut my body with a knife I don't mind, provided you can cure me. " —" Very well! stand there, put your head through the window, and look if more persons pass to the right or to the left, but don't look behind you, for if you do, my medicine

will have no effect, and you will die in a fortnight. "

Whilst the young girl, obedient to these instructions, was looking into the street, the old woman opened her legs, " Lean a little more on the sill of the window, " she said, " and do not turn round; I am going to rub you with some tar ointment. " Then in a low voice she called her nephew. " Now then, set to work. "

The lad came behind the young girl, and shoved in his ointment four *vershoks* deep. Feeling the remedy act, the patient began to wag her arse. "Granny, dear granny, " she cried, " rub me — rub me some more with that tar ointment ! " Grigori, his business being done, retired behind the stove. " Well, my daughter, " said the old woman, " now you look well and fresh. " The peasant girl thanked her warmly. " Thank you, granny ! That is a capital remedy. It is like a real charm! "

—" My medicines never do any harm, and this one

is very good for women and girls. But which way did you see most people pass? " —" To the right, granny. " —" Ah! you are lucky! Go home, and may God protect you! "

The girl went away, and the young man also took his departure. After dinner he took his mare to drink at the brook. The peasant girl saw him, and ran towards him, crying: " Ah! *matouchka!* my dove. " — " Oh! granny, dear granny, rub me some more with your tar ointment! " replied Grigori laughingly. At this the peasant girl bit her lips, and after that lived on good terms with the young man.

ANOTHER VERSION

A young man was accustomed to pass before the house of a merchant, and when opposite to it, to cough and spit, and then say " I am stuffed up with eating too much goose. " One day the merchant's daughter said to him: " My father has plenty of money, but he does not eat goose every day, " — " Riches do not always give happiness," replied the other, and he returned home. The merchant's daughter called to an old beggar woman: " Follow that young man, " she said, " and find out what he eats for his dinner, and you shall be well rewarded when you bring me the information. "

When the young man arrived home, the beggar woman who had followed him, asked his leave to rest a bit in the *izba*, and she was allowed to come in. The greatest poverty prevailed in the house. " Mother, " said the young man, " is there anything to eat in the house? " — " There is some *shchi* left from yesterday, and some *kasha* from the day before yesterday. " — " Give me the *kasha*. " — The mother brought in the dish, and said there was no butter. — " Can you give me a bit of lard, then? " — " No, but here is a bit of candle. " He mixed this with his *kasha*, and began to eat it greedily.

The begger woman related all this to the merchant's daughter. Soon afterwards the young man again passed before the merchant's house; he coughed, spat, and uttered the usual phrase : " I am stuffed up with eating too much goose. " — " He has eaten *kasha* with a candle in it, " cried the merchant's daughter out of the window. —" May the devil take her! How did she know that? It must certainly have been the beggar woman who told her."

He set out to look for this woman, and when he found her, said: " Can you manage this business for me and when I have some money I will pay you? " — " Very well, " said the old woman, and she went at once to the merchant's daughter: " How are you, miss? " —" I am very ill, granny, I always have pains in my belly;

is there any way of curing that? " — " Yes, get
ready a warm bath, and I will rub your belly
with some grease. " —The bath was prepared,
and the old woman who had previously hidden
the young man in the room, brought the merchant's daughter there, undressed her, and when
she was quite naked, said: " Now, my dear, I
must cover your eyes, or you will feel ill. " The
old woman tied a handkerchief over the invalid's eyes, and laid her upon a bench. " Now, " she
said, " I am going to rub you with a little
grease, " and she passed her hand twice over the
young girl's belly. " Now, it is going to be a
little harder. " Then, at a sign from the woman,
the young man approached the merchant's daughter, and attacked her so furiously that she uttered
loud cries. " Have a little courage, my dear. At
first, it always hurts, but it is over in a minute,
and then all will be right, and your belly will
be cured. "

The girl soon found the treatment to her
liking. " Rub me, granny, " she said, "rub me!
Your grease is very good. " The operation being
finished, the young man returned to his hiding
place, and the old woman took the bandage off
the eyes of the merchant's daughter. The girl
saw that there was some blood under her. " What
is that, granny? " —" That is some bad blood
that came out of you; now you will be better. "
—" Yes, granny. That is a capital ointment; it

is sweeter than honey. Won't you rub me again? " —" Do you want it again? " —" Oh, yes, granny! my belly begins to hurt me again! " The old woman again bandaged her eyes, and laid her upon the bench, and the young man again set to work. " Rub, granny! Rub! Your ointment is excellent, " said the merchant's daughter. As soon as he had finished his work, the young man went away. The invalid rose: " Granny, " she said, "bring me some of that and here is a hundred rubles for your trouble. " So ended the affair.

When the young man next passed before the merchant's house, he began as usual to say: " I am stuffed up with eating too much goose. " To which the girl replied by crying out of the window: " He ate candle grease with his *kasha*. " And the youth retorted, " Rub, granny, rub, your ointment is excellent! "

Soon however the girl's waist began to enlarge to an abnormal extent, and her mother noticed it. " Why is it, my child, that you never go out of the house, and that your belly has become so big? " — " Oh, mother, do you know that it is ever since that good old woman took me to the baths. She rubbed my belly with some ointment; — such nice ointment, sweeter than honey. " The mother guessed the truth; so she sent for the beggar-woman, and questioned her. " You took my daughter to the bath, and rubbed her with some ointment? " —" Yes, madam." —" Rub me, also. " —" Willingly. " — She ran off at once to the young man. " Dress yourself, and come quickly; the merchant's wife wants to be greased. " They went to the public baths. The old woman bandaged the eyes of the merchant's wife, and laid her upon a bench, and the young man treated her as he had treated her daughter. In the middle of the operation, the merchant's wife suddenly tore the bandage from off her eyes, and saw the young man. She kissed him to reward him for his trouble. " My lad, " she said, " I have been married twenty years, and I have never enjoyed myself so much. Here are a hundred rubles for you, and you shall marry my daughter. " — The young man married the rich heiress, and there was a grand dinner on the occasion; I was there myself, and drank wine and mead and everybody had as much as he wanted to eat and drink!

ANOTHER VERSION

A certain soldier was addicted to drink; he also suffered from asthma, and therefore went to an old woman who practised medicine. Although she was advanced in years, this woman was still of an ardent temperament. When she saw the soldier, she felt an itching between her

legs. " What is you want, soldier? " — " I am
asthmatical, and I came to ask you to cure me. "
— " Undress yourself and sit down." — The
soldier obeyed, and the woman placed before
him a bottle of brandy. — " Drink, soldier, as
much as you like. " — The visitor did not need
pressing, and soon showed signs of drunkenness;
finally, he fell on the floor, and went fast asleep.

Then the old woman began to fumble about,
first passing her hand over his navel, and then
lower still. " Ah, I am astonished, " she cried,
sadly. " I have made a pretty mistake. So far
from having given him any energy, his member
is quite limp. " —She laid the sleeper on the
bed, lay down by his side, and tried by tickling
and rubbing to induce some signs of virility in
the soldier; but he continued to snore like an
organ pipe. After having made one final attempt,
the old woman fell asleep also.

A little before dawn, the soldier awoke, and
seeing a woman sleeping by his side, said to
himself. " Shall I have a turn? " and set to work
to roger her. The cunning old woman, awakened
thus out of her sleep, feigned indignation. " What
are you doing, soldier? Are you not ashamed of
yourself? " But as she thus spoke she assumed
a position which would facilitate the operation.
" Why, granny, is it bad for a sick man? If
so I will get off. " — " What nonsense you
are talking, soldier! On the contrary, shove

ıt in as far as you can; it will do you good. "
When he had rogered the old woman, the soldier
went away, saying to himself. " I do not know
whether it will do me good, but I wanted it. "

Unfortunately for him, there was sleeping in
the loft a young girl, the niece of the old woman,
who had witnessed the scene, and related it to
the girls of her acquaintance, and from that
time the soldier was the butt of all their sar-
casms. " He made love to the old woman! He
made love to the old woman! " was buzzed in
his ears unceasingly. At last he was out of
patience, and went and related his griefs to his
mistress of a night. " Oh, my benefactor, " she
replied, " why did you not tell me before?
I would soon have made those chatterers cease
their teasing! Oh, the young dolts! Is not an
old woman's slit as good as theirs? What right
have they to make fun of us thus? Listen, soldier; I am often visited by a young girl I am
treating for a rupture. Come here tomorrow
night, and hide yourself in the bed. I will tell
the girl to go down on her hands and knees,
and then you can give her good measure! "

The next day, at the hour named the soldier
went to the old woman's house, and hid himself
in her bed. In less than half an hour the girl arrived, as soon as the soldier saw her, his member
stood erect. The old woman examined her patient,
and said: " My dear, there is a nest of fleas

between your legs. There is no means of taking them away except with the hand, but if they are left there you will die. " —" Granny, be good enough to rid me of them, I beg. " — " Well, then there is no other means! I did not want to put my hand down there, but it must be done! Here is a handkerchief; bind your eyes, take off your clothes, and go down on your hands and knees. "

The girl did as she was ordered; after which the soldier approached her, took his member in both hands and introduced it into her gap. The patient began to cry out: " That hurts me, granny! That hurts me! " —" Have a little courage, my dear. These cursed fleas have multiplied so exceedingly, that they are even in the orifice! " The soldier penetrated to the depth of four *vershoks*, and there were fresh cries. " Oh, granny, I shall die. It hurts me, granny, it hurts me. " — " Wait a minute, my child, I will put on a little tar ointment, and then perhaps you will feel better. " The soldier pushed in as far as he could, and the girl bit her tongue; but, at last, feeling the effect of the grease, she cried: " Ah, granny, now that is nice! Really that does me good. Can't you rub me again with your ointment? I feel quite revived, I will get a whole jar of tar from my father and bring it to you. " —On hearing these words the soldier used all his efforts to satisfy the girl and worked so well that he considerably enlarged the opening by which he had entered. "Do you feel any relief? " asked the old woman; " it seems to me that now they are all smashed. " —" Oh, granny, now I feel much better. " The soldier then hid himself; the invalid got up, put on her clothes, and went away.

The next day, the girl, who was now as large as a funnel met the soldier, and began to tease him: " He performed on the old woman! He performed on the old woman " ! — " But it is better with tar ointment, " he replied:

LIII

The wonderful whistle.

In a certain country there lived a villager who was wretchedly poor. One day the *barine* sent for him, and said: " Listen, *moujik*! You pay no rent, and you have nothing to seize, to pay your debts you must serve me three years. " The peasant passed one year, then two, then three in the service of the *barine*, and the latter saw that the *moujik* would soon be free, and said to himself: " What pretext can I find to keep this serf in my service another three years? " He called the *moujik*, and spoke to him in these words: " Listen, *moujik*: Here are ten hares, take them out to feed in the country, but have a care not to lose one, for if you do, you will remain three years more in my service. " The *moujik* had no sooner let loose the hares in the field, than they ran away in all directions. " What is to be done? " he thought. " Now I am really lost, " and he sat down and began to cry.

Suddenly an old man appeared before him: " Why are you weeping, *moujik*? " he asked, " Why should I not weep, old man? My master charged me to feed some hares, and they have all run away, and now I am a ruined man. " — The old man gave him a whistle, and said: " You

have but to play on this instrument, and you
will see them all run up to you. " The peasant
thanked him, took the whistle, and had no sooner began to play than all the hares ran towards
him. He took them all back to his master, who
counted them, and satisfied himself there was
not one missing. " Well, what is to be done? "
said the *barine* to his wife. " How can we catch
this *moujik* napping? " —" I have an idea, my
friend. Tomorrow whilst he is feeding his hares,
I will come to him in a disguise and buy one. " —
" Very good: that will do. "

The next morning the *moujik* left the village
with the hares, and the moment he approached
the wood, they all ran away — some one way,
some another. As to the *moujik*, he sat down on
the ground, and began to plait some bark shoes.
Soon there came a lady in a carriage, which stopped, and the lady alighted, and came to the peasant. " What are you doing here, *moujik* ? " —
" I am feeding cattle. " — " What cattle? " —
He took his whistle and as soon as he began to
use it all the hares gathered round him. " Ah,
moujik, " said the lady; " sell me a little hare! "
—" That is quite impossible, they belong to
my master, and he is very severe. He would be
capable of killing and eating me. " —The *barinia* persisted. "Let me have one I beg. " Seeing
how much she desired a hare, the *moujik* replied
" I have made a vow, madam " — " What vow? "

— " To give a hare to the person who would let me futter her. " —" Take money instead of that, moujik. " — " No, I will not accept any other terms. " Tired of discussing the matter, she reluctantly consented to this condition; the *moujik*

rogered her, and gave her a hare : " Only, madam, " he said, " be sure and hold it gently or you will strangle it. "

She took the hare, stepped into her carriage and prepared to return home, but the *moujik* had but to sound a few notes on his whistle, and the animal escaped out of the hands of the *bari-*

nia and returned to him. When the lady arrived
at home, her husband asked her: " Well, did you
buy a hare? " —" Certainly I bought one, but
at the first sound of the *moujik's* whistle, the
hare jumped out of the carriage, and I never saw
it again. "

The next day the *barinia* again went to the
peasant, and the same scene was enacted as on the
previous day. " What are you doing, *moujik*? "
— " I am plaiting bark shoes and minding my
master's herds. " — " Where is this herd? " —
The *moujik* played on his whistle, and the hares
immediately ran to him. The *barinia* expressed
a wish to buy one of the hares. " I have made a
vow, " he replied. " What is it? " —" Let me futter you. " The lady consented, and in return
received a hare, but, as soon as the sound of the
whistle was heard, the animal ran away from
her.

The third day the *barine* himself arrived in a
carriage. " What are you doing, *moujik*? " —
" Minding cattle whilst they graze. " — " But
where are your cattle? " The *moujik* sounded his
whistle, and the hares ran to him. " Sell me
one. " — " Not for money: I have made a vow. "
— " What vow? " — " To anyone who will futter a
mare, I will give a hare. " — The *barine* committed an unnatural offence with a mare. The
moujik gave him a hare, and said: " Hold it
gently *barine*, or you may strangle it. " The

barine took the hare, but when he was driving
away in his carriage, the peasant began to blow
his whistle: the call was heard by the animal,
which jumped out of the carriage and returned
to its place amongst the others. The *barine*, finding all his plans fail, gave the peasant his liberty.

LIV

The shepherd.

In a village there lived a shepherd who was a
great favorite with all the girls and young wom-
en of the locality. But though he was willing
enough to make love, he would not do it to everybody. This caused him to be hated by some of

the peasant girls, and rightly or wrongly they set about the report that he had been surprised in a very equivocal position with a mare, and ever after that the lad was a butt for the jokes of all the young people of the village. The most bitter of all against him was a girl named Dounia. In the morning, when he was taking his cattle to pasture, she would cry to him: " Oh, Ivan, take care of my mare! " The young man took note of all this.

There lived also in the village a good-natured old woman whom the young girls were accustomed to visit in the evening. The shepherd threw himself at her feet: " Granny, " he said, " do something for me, and I will ever pray to God for you, and will never forget you as long as I live. " Then he related to her all his troubles, and gave her a silver ruble. " Very well, my friend; come to me at nightfall. "

In the evening the shepherd brought back his flock out of the field; it rained a little; the women also brought in their cattle, and Dounia amongst others went to look for her cow. The old woman saw her through the window, and called to her, " Dounia, Dounia, come here!" The girl quickly came and the old woman began to scold her severely; the shepherd was in her house, hidden behind the stove. " Take care Douniacha you will repent when it is too late. "

These words frightened Dounia, who did not

know of what fault she had been guilty. " Foolish, imprudent girl that you are, " continued
the old woman: " You run about boldly, and
jump over ditches without thinking of the conse-
quences! And what have you gained by acting
thus? I will tell you, little fool, what you have
done: You have damaged your honor! Who do
you think will marry you now? " — " Oh,
granny, is there no means of mending it? " —
" Heu! Mend it! Of course it's the poor old
granny who is asked to do every hard job. Come
here, do what I tell you and screw up your courage for the operation will be painful. " — " Very
well, granny! " — " Look through the window
and open your legs; but don't turn your head,
or the remedy will fail and there will be no hope
for you. "

Having thus spoken, the old woman tucked up
the girl's *sarafane* and made a sign to the shepherd. Ivan came up gently, took off his trousers, and set to work to mend Dounia's honor.
— " Well, is it good, " asked the old woman.
— " Oh, yes, granny, it is good! Mend it again
granny! I will never forget you! " —When the
shepherd had finished his business, he again
slipped behind the stove. —" Now, " said the
old woman, " return home, little fool, and pray
to God for your granny. "

On the morrow, when he took his flock out to
graze, Dounia again began to tease the shepherd

by allusions to the mare. — " Do you want me
to mend your honor? " he replied. — " Oh,
that is not good of you, Ivan, " said the young
girl, reproachfully. — " I don't know how you
found it, but to me it seemed very good indeed, " replied the shepherd.

LV

The soldier, the peasant, and the girl.

Some soldiers had been quartered in a village,
and the peasant women became very familiar
with them, and naturally these relations were
not quite innocent; whilst the master of the
house was working in the fields, his wife ate,
drank, and lay with the soldier who was quartered on the household.

One of the *moujiks* had a wife of very de-
praved habits; many times had he found her either with peasants or soldiers, but she had always
managed to find some excuse. On one occasion,
the husband surprised her with a young man in
a stable. " Well, you whore, what have you to
say now? " As the young man was then on the
top of her, all she could reply was: " Forgive
me, my dear. " — But she quickly got up, ran
to the house, and came weeping, to her mother-
in-law. Very soon the husband arrived. " I

would not believe what people told me, mother, but now I myself found her in the stable with a young man. " — " You hear, mother, " sobbed the woman, " what calumnious accusations are brought against me. " — " Why, you cursed whore! did I not find you, only a few minutes ago, lying under Andreiouchka! " " You lie, scoundrel! Well! If so, tell me where my head was? " — The *moujik* was puzzled, and ended by saying: " The devil only knows where your head was. " — " You see, mother, what false accusations he brings against me! " The old woman was very indignant with her son, and reproached him bitterly. " Very good, " said the *moujik*, " I shall catch you again soon, my dear! "

Some time after that, this peasant woman had struck up an acquaintance with a soldier. The soldier laid the woman on a truss of straw, and began to roger her. The husband, who had his suspicions, went to the stable, and surprised the couple *in flagrante delicto*. — " Ah, soldier, that is not right of you! " — " Between you two, the devil himself would not know what to do, " replied the soldier. She says that it *is* all right, and you say that it is *not* right. There's no satisfying both of you. " — " Soldier, I shall demand justice against you. " — " Very well! demand it; I have already obtained it. "

LVI

The soldier who slept whilst his cock worked.

A *moujik* was married to a young wife. Some soldiers were quartered in the village, and one of them was sent to lodge at the cottage of this peasant. When night came they all three lay down on the same bed; the woman in the middle, and a man on each side of her. The *moujik* talked to his wife, and the soldier, taking advantage of a favorable opportunity, attacked his hostess from the rear. The peasant also wished to futter his wife, and began to fumble her about, and on putting his hand on her slit, he found it occupied. " What are you doing, soldier? " — Then the soldier began to snore, as though he were in a deep sleep. " Ah, what a queer man that soldier is," observed the *moujik*: " he is fast asleep, and he has stuffed his lance into my wife's slit. " — " I beg your pardon, host! I don't know by what chance it came there! "

ANOTHER VERSION

A soldier after having long sought by what means he could enjoy a woman of Little Russia, hit on the following stratagem. He said to the husband, with whom he lodged, " My host, there are a lot of devils in your house; they will not let me sleep. How do you sleep? " — " I sleep well, thank God. " — " Very well, then I will sleep with you. " — " Let him sleep with us, " said the woman. The husband consented, and took his place at the outside of the bed, and put his wife in the middle, with her face turned towards him. As to the soldier, he was put in the corner, and very soon began to assail the mistress of the house from behind. The husband, putting out his hand softly, caught hold of the soldier's prickle. " Aha, Mr. Soldier! He is asleep, but that does not prevent him from introducing his tool into a slit that does not belong to him. " — " What are you doing, son of a devil, " cried the soldier, " Why do you lay hold of my tool? I would not allow your wife to do that, much less you! " — " And why Mr. Soldier, do you shove your tool into a coynte that does not belong to you? " — " But did it enter there? " — " I should think so, I had a good deal of trouble to get it out again. " — " What a bold scoundrel! I will give him a sharp lesson, and teach him not to shove himself into a hole where he has no business! "

LVII

The soldier and the woman of Little Russia.

A native of Little Russia was on his road to town with his wife and son, in a cart drawn by oxen, and saw a cuirassier ramming his mare, which was fastened to a tree by the side of the road. — " What are you doing, soldier? " — " This horse that the Government gave me has put its leg out, and I am setting it again. " —The woman said to herself: " Certainly he has a big tool! Why he is futtering the mare! " — She cunningly sat herself on the edge of the cart and when the wheel met with a rut she was tipped out. —" Run quickly and find the soldier," she cried, " I have dislocated one of my limbs! " —In a few seconds the husband came up to the cuirassier. " Soldier, be a father to us! Come and help us please! My wife has dislocated one of her limbs. " —" Of course, I will come, since you are in trouble I am bound to help you. " Thereupon the husband led the soldier to the scene of the accident.

The Little Russian woman lay on the ground and groaned: " Oh Lord I have broken my leg! " —" Have you a tarpaulin for the cart? " asked the soldier of the husband. — " Yes. " — " Very

good, give it to me. " He covered over the cart
and lifted the victim of the accident into the
vehicle. " Have you some bread and salt? " he
asked. —" Yes. " — The cuirassier took a bit
of bread and sprinkled salt over it. " Now, Little
Russian, you hold the oxen so that they do not
move. " The Little Russian held them by the
horns and meanwhile the soldier climbed into the
cart and began to roger the woman. The son noticed that the soldier was on the top of his mother. " Papa, " he cried, " Papa! The soldier is rogering mamma. " — " Truly, my son, one would
think that he was rogering her. But no! He
could not do that after eating our bread and salt. "
— When the cuirassier had finished his business,
he got out of the cart, and the woman said to
him: " Thank you soldier; here is a silver
ruble for you. " — The husband also in his
turn pulled his purse out of his pocket and
gave two rubles to the soldier. — " Thank
you soldier for having cured my wife. "

LVIII

The soldier and the Little Russian.

A soldier who lodged in the house of a Little
Russian had an intrigue with the wife of his
host. The man perceiving this left off working

in the fields and did not leave the house. The soldier therefore had recourse to a trick; he changed his dress and came one evening and knocked at the window of the *izba*. " Who is there? " asked the Little Russian woman. —" It is Babe, " replied this soldier. — " Who is Babe? " — " The man who futters the Little Russians! Is the master of the house at home? " — " What do you want of him? " — " An order has been issued to futter all the Little Russians! Open the door quickly! " — The husband who heard these words did not know where to hide himself, he caught up a cloak, wrapped himself in it and hid under a bench.

The woman opened the door and the soldier entered, crying: " Where is the master of the house? " — " He is not at home. " — The soldier began to look in the stove, in the loft and in all the corners; at last something under the bench attracted his attention. " What is that? " — " It is a calf, " replied the woman. With that the Little Russian began to low like the animal he was supposed to be. — " Very well! Since the master of the house is absent, you must take his place. Lie down there! " — " Oh, Lord! Can't you wait till my husband comes back ? " — " How do you think I can wait? I have to visit every house in the village, and if I omit only one, I shall get three-hundred blows of the stick on my back. Lie down at once, I have no time to stop here talking to you. " The Little Russian gave herself up to the caresses of the soldier, who pressed her so hard that he made her fart. When he had futtered her he went away.

The husband then came out of his hiding-place. " Wife, " he said, " I thank you for the trouble you have taken for me. You could not contain yourself and began to fart, but I am sure that, if it had been my case, I should have s .. t myself. Oh, wife you are very clever, but I am more clever than you; you, only spoke of the calf, whilst I lowed like a real calf! "

LIX

The deserter.

A deserter hid himself in a peasant's barn to pass the night, and lay down on the hay. Just as he was going to sleep he heard footsteps. The soldier, being frightened, climbed up into the roof. A girl, followed by a young man, entered the barn, they brought with them a bottle of brandy and some victuals, and after they had placed the provisions in a corner, they undressed, and began to embrace. Then the young man threw his companion down on the hay, and rogered her. " Ah, my dear, " said the girl, whilst she was cuddling her lover, " If, by God's will, I should have a baby, who will take care of it? " — " There is one above us who will take care of it, " replied the young man. At hearing this, the soldier could not contain his

indignation. " Oh, you rascals! " he cried, " do you expect me to support the fruits of your filthy fornication? " Terrified in the midst of their pleasure by this unexpected reply, the two lovers ran away as fast as they could. The soldier slipped to the ground, gathered up all their clothes, and the provisions they had brought, and then started off on his way again.

LX

The soldier and the *pope*.

A soldier wanted to futter the wife of a *pope*; but how was he to manage it? He put on his uniform, took his musket, and went to the priest's house. " *Batouchka*, a new ukase has just been issued ordering all the *popes* to be futtered, prepare yourself! " — "Oh, soldier, cannot you make an exception in my favor? " — " What an absurd idea! Do you think I am going to get punished to please you? Be sharp, and take off your trousers, and put yourself in position? " — " But look here soldier: Cannot my wife take my place? " — " Yes, that can be done! But no one must know about it, or it will be the worse for me. Besides, what will you give me, *batouchka*? I will not accept less than a hundred rubles. "— " Take them, soldier, but have pity upon me. " — " All right! lie down on your face in the cart, and let your wife lie on your back. I will get on her, and then it will look as though I were rogering you. "

The pope lay down in the cart, and his wife

placed herself on the top of him; then the soldier lifted up the *popadia's* dress and began to futter her. As the operation lasted a long time, it naturally caused the *pope*, who was lying on the bottom of the cart, to become violently excited, his lance stood so strongly that it knocked a hole in the bottom of the cart, and came out, all red, on the other side. At this sight the *pope's* daughter cried: " Oh, what a strong tool that soldier has. It has gone right through my mother and my father, and the tip of it is still wagging. "

LXI

The soldier's wedding present.

A rich peasant married off his son and gave a grand dinner on the occasion. At night the young couple were put to bed, and the following morning, when they awoke, the usual felicitations were bestowed upon them, then they were covered with a white sheet, on which were placed the wedding presents, everybody giving according to his means.

All gave something, except a soldier, who lay, drunk, on the floor. The old man called to him: " Come soldier, give a present to the young couple! " The soldier rose. " So be it, " he said,

" Here is my present! " and without stopping
to put on his trousers, he lifted up the sheet and
attacked the bride from behind. " Soldier! "
cried the father-in-law, " That is not the way to
give a wedding present. " Then said the bride,
" No matter, papa, it is very good all the same. "
The father-in-law was vexed, and said to the
girls: " Make this soldier ashamed of his conduct. " — " Oh, soldier, " cried all the girls in
chorus, " You have been to all parts of the
world, and do not know to give a wedding present. — " What stupid women you are, " he
replied, " I made such gift as I could. "

LXII

The mother-in-law and the foolish
son-in-law.

A peasant lived with his wife; they had one
daughter, a young man asked and obtained her
hand in marriage. At Christmas-time, the son-
in-law came to see his mother-in-law. She invited him to sit at the table, placed before him
various dishes, and entered into conversation
with him. " Tell me, my son, " she asked, " what
cattle you killed for the feast at your home? "
— " Well, the evening before the festival, my

father found a bitch in the *ambar* (1) and beat
it till he made it piss and s..t. The bitch at
last made its escape, but my father went after
it, caught it just as it was running out of the
house and beat it again on the vulva. " — " Ah,
I have a clever son-in-law, " thought the mother-
in-law. " He has plenty of wit. You don't catch
me asking him anything again. "

LXIII

The talkative wife.

A peasant wished to assure himself that he
could if necessary rely upon his wife's discretion.
One day, when he wished to satisfy a personal
want, he went into the courtyard, and when he

(1) The place where corn, flour, and other provisions
are kept.

had relieved himself, returned to the house;
then he sat on a bench, bowed his head, and
began to utter deep sighs, like a man with a
troubled conscience. His wife questioned him.
" What is the matter? Are you ill? Just now
you were so gay, and now you are quite sad. "
— " Be quiet, wife, " replied the *moujik*, " I myself
do not know whether to augur good or evil from
what has happened to me. " — The woman persisted. " Speak, tell me what has occurred. " —
" Just now, wife, I went to the privy, and just
as I began, a crow flew out of my arse. I want
to know what that means! "

As soon as the peasant woman had heard this
story, she made some pretext for running off to
one of her cronies, to whom she hastened to
say: " Have you heard, my dear, what happened to my husband? Yesterday he went to the
privy, and hardly had he commenced to relieve
himself than two crows flew out of his arse.
What can that signify? " — After they had long
discussed this mysterious occurrence, the two
women took leave of each other. The crony went
at once to one of her friends, and said: " Do
you know, my dear Arina, what has happened
to Ivan? His wife came to see me, and told me
that when he went to the stool, three crows flew
out of his arse. " Arina at once informed her
neighbors that when Ivan went to the privy,
four crows came out of him.

As the story was spread abroad, the number
of crows went on increasing; and when it had
been all round the village, it was stated that
twelve crows had flown out of Ivan's arse, and
he became quite a local celebrity. He did not
dare to show himself abroad, for every one he
met asked him: " Is it true, my friend, that
twelve crows flew out of your arse? Tell me
all about it! "

LXIV

The *pope* who neighed like a stallion.

In a village there lived a *pope* who was very
fond of women; whenever he saw from his window a young woman pass his door, he would
lean out of the window, and begin to neigh like
a stallion. In the same village there lived a *moujik* who was married to a very pretty woman.
Every day, when she went to fetch water, she
passed before the *pope's* house, and as soon as
the priest saw her, he put his head out of the
window, and began to neigh.

One day, when she came home the woman said
to her husband, " Tell me, my little man, I beg,
why it is that the *pope* neighs like a horse whenever I pass his house, as I go to fetch water ?"
— " Why, you fool, it is because he has taken a

fancy to you. But you do as I tell you, and when you go to fetch water, and the *pope* begins to " hi, ho, ho, " you reply, " hi, hi, hi. " Then he will come running out to you, and ask you to sleep with him. Induce him to come to the house, and we will treat him in such a way that he will never want to neigh again. " The woman took a pitcher, and went to draw some water. The *pope* saw her through the window, and filled the street with his " hi, ho ho! " —" Hi, hi, hi. " replied the woman. The *pope* hastily put on a coat, ran out of his house, and came up to the woman. " Well, *matouchka*, can you manage that for me? " " Yes, *batouchka*, my husband is about to go to the fair; but he cannot find any horses. " —" Why did you not say so before? Send him to me, and I will lend him my two horses and my carriage, and he can go to the town and transact his business! "

The woman returned home, and told her husband of this offer. He went to the *pope*, who had been awaiting him a long time. " Be good enough, *batouchka*, to lend me your cart and horses to go to the fair. " — " Willingly my friend, willingly. " The peasant returned home with the *pope's* cart and horses, and said to his wife: " Now, mistress, I am going just beyond the village. I will remain there a little time, and then come back. During that time, the *pope* is free to come and amuse himself here. When I come back, and he hears me knock at the door, he will be frightened, and will beg of you to show him a hiding place. Put him in the chest where we keep the soot, do you understand? " — " Very good. "

The *moujik* mounted the cart, and drove outside the village. The *pope*, seeing him go, ran at once to the woman's house. " Good day, *matouchka*. " — " Good day, *batouchka*. Now we are free to enjoy ourselves. Sit down to the table, and drink some brandy. " After he had drunk a small glassful, the *pope*, who could no longer restrain himself, took off his cassock, his boots, and his socks but just as he was going to get into bed, there was a knock at the door. " Who is that knocking, *matouchka?* " asked the *pope* in a frightened voice. " Ah, *batouchka*, it is my husband who has returned, no doubt he has forgotten something. " — " But where can I hide myself, my dear. " — " There is in that corner an empty box, get inside that. " The *pope* quickly got in, and fell all amongst the soot, and there he lay, more dead than alive. The woman made haste to close the lid, and then turned the key in the lock.

The *moujik* walked into the *izba*. " Why have you come back? " asked his wife. — " I forgot to take the soot-box. Perhaps I shall be able to sell the soot at the fair. Help me to put it into the cart. The man and his wife lifted up the chest

which contained the *pope,* and set to work to drag it out of the *izba.* " Why is it so heavy? " said the husband. "I thought it was nearly empty, and it is a good weight. " — Whilst he was lugging about the heavy box, he purposely knocked it against the wall and the door. " Oh, I am caught in a nice trap! " thought the *pope* as he was thus knocked about. At last the chest was hoisted into the cart, and the peasant sat on the top of it, and set out for the town.

He lashed the horses, and they set off at full gallop. On the road he met the carriage of a *barine,* which was coming in the opposite direction. " Go and tell that *moujik* to stop, " the gentleman ordered his lackey, " and ask him why he is driving so furiously. " The lackey ran forward, and cried: " Hi! *Moujik!* Stop ! Stop ! " The peasant obeyed. " My master wants to know whv you are driving at such a rate. " — " I am hunting for devils: that is why I am going at full gallop. " — " And have you caught any, *moujik*? " — " Yes, I have caught one, and I was pursuing another when you interrupted me, and now I shall not be able to overtake him: "

When the lackey reported these words to his master, the *barine* came at once to the peasant. " My friend, show me the devil you have caught: I have never seen one in all my life. " — " Give me a hundred rubles, *barine,* and I will show it to you. " — " All right. " The gentleman gave the hundred rubles, and the *moujik* opened the chest, and showed its contents. The *pope* lay there all bruised, and blackened with soot, and his hair all disordered. " Oh, how ugly he is, " said the *barine*. " He is really a devil! He has long hair and a black skin, and his eyes are starting out of his head! " Then the *moujik* shut up the chest, and continued his journey.

When he arrived at the town he drove to the field where the fair was held. " What have you to sell, *moujik?* " he was asked. — " A devil, " he replied. — " How much do you ask for him? " — " A thousand rubles? " — " Nothing less? " — " Nothing less, a thousand rubles is the fixed price. " Such a crowd collected round the peasant, that an apple thrown amongst them would not have fallen to the ground. Two rich merchants pushing a passage through the crowd as well as they could approached the cart. " *Moujik*, will you sell us your devil? " — " I only await a purchaser. " — " Well, what is your price? " — " A thousand rubles, and that is without the chest, for I want the chest. If I catch another devil, I must have somewhere to put him. " The merchants decided to go halves in the speculation, and handed a thousand rubles to the *moujik*. " Come, and take possession of your devil, " said he, and opened the chest. Immediately, the pope jumped out and ran through the crowd, which fled in all directions. " What an awful devil! If we should meet one like that, we should be killed, " said one of the merchants to the other.

As to the *moujik*, he returned home, and took the horses back to the priest's house. " Many thanks for your cart, *batouchka*, " he said. " I did an excellent stroke of business at the fair, and gained a thousand good rubles. " His wife went soon afterwards to draw some water, and as she passed the *pope's* house, she saw him and began to go " hi, hi, hi. " — " Be quiet, cursed wretch! " replied the priest, " With your hi, hi, hi, your husband has played me a scurvy trick. From that day the *pope* was never heard to neigh any more.

ANOTHER VERSION

In a certain country there lived a *pope* who was in love with the wife of a peasant. Whenever he saw her going to fetch water, he would begin to neigh like a stallion. One day, when she was, as usual, going to the well, the *pope* began to neigh when he saw her, and she replied in the same manner. In an instant the priest was by her side. " Well, my charmer, I should like to make your acquaintance. " — " Very well, *batouchka*; but I must make my arrangements. " — When she returned home, the woman said to her husband: " The *pope* wants to pass the night with me. " — " Well, let him come. I will go to work in the fields and on my return I will catch him; perhaps we may get something out of him. "

The *moujik* started off in his cart, and purposely passed in front of the *pope's* house. " Where are you going, friend? " — " I am going to work in the fields, *batouchka*; give me your blessing. " — " It is a good deed, " replied the *pope*; " May God bless you. " A little later, the woman went to fetch water, and meeting the *pope*, said to

him: " My husband has gone to work in the fields. Come this evening, *batouchka*! I will prepare a feast for you, but do you bring some brandy. "

The *pope* awaited the evening impatiently, and as soon as it was dark, he quickly dressed himself put some money and a bottle of brandy in his pocket and ran off to the peasant's house. " Good day, my charmer, " said he as he entered. " Good day, *batouchka*! " — The visitor drew from his pocket a bottle of brandy, and placed it on the table. They ate and drank as much as they wished, and then the *pope* began to play with the woman, and feel her breasts, but just as he was pushing her towards the bed, a knock was heard at the window. " Open, wife! Why is the house shut up? Have you a lover with you! " — " Wait a bit, my little man, and I will open the door. "

The *pope* was frightened. " What will become of me? Where can I hide myself? " —
" Undress yourself quickly. *batouchka*, " replied
the mistress of the house; put on these old rags,
and sit down near the stove. If my husband questions me about you I will say: It is a beggar
who asked a night's shelter, which I granted
him. " The *pope* immediately took off his cassock, put on the rags, and sat near the stove.
The *moujik* entered the *izba*. " Why have you
come back so soon, little man? You told me that
you had gone for three days. " — " I forgot to
take a barrel of water with me. Who is that
man there? " — " He is a poor traveller. He
asked hospitality for the night, and I took him
in. " — " All right, mistress, serve supper, and
then we will go to bed, tomorrow I must get up
early and go to work. " The peasant sat down at
the table and began to eat greedily. " Perhaps
you would like some brandy? " said his wife. —
" Is there any in the house? " —" Yes, I went
to see my mother today, and she gave me a
whole bottle. " The peasant drank several
glasses of spirits, then he said to the *pope*. " Sit
down there, comrade, and sup with us. " The
priest took his seat at the table but remained
silent. " Eh, wife, this fellow begs for alms, but
his beard covers all his face and he is ashamed
to show himself to honest people; see how
frightened he is! Give me a pair of scissors
and I will clip his beard. " The woman brought

scissors and the peasant cut the *pope's* beard close to his chin.

A little later, a new idea came to the *moujik*. " Eh, mistress, " he said, " go to the *pope's* wife, and ask her to come and eat a bit with us. She is a nice woman, and we ought to feast her. " The wife ran to the priest's house, and the *popadia*, delighted at the invitation, quitted her bed, dressed herself, and came to the *moujik's* hut. " Why did you not come sooner, *matouchka*? " he asked. " Oh, you know a *pope's* wife takes some time to make her toilette. Whilst she is washing and dressing a good *moujik* might travel ten *versts*. (1) " " Well, sit down, *matouchka*, and sup with us and take pot-luck. It is a feast with us today, for our cow has calved. " Thereupon he poured out for his visitor a large glass of brandy, which was followed by a second, and then a third. " Drink, *matouchka*, to the health of our calf. " — Soon there was no more brandy left. " Wife, " ordered the *moujik*, " Go to the inn and bring another half-bottle; today I am going to enjoy myself. "

The woman went to the inn, and the *moujik*, seeing the *pope's* wife was drunk, began to make love to her. At first, his requests were energetically refused, but he persisted till at last she gave in. " Do let me, I beg, *matouchka*, " he

(1) A Russian unit of distance. About two-thirds of a mile.

said supplicatingly. " I have never tried a *pope's* wife. " — " But where shall we conceal ourselves? " she replied. " There is a beggar here. " — " That doesn't matter, let him look on! " he answered; then he laid the *popadia* on the bed, and began to futter her under the eyes of the *pope*, who uttered deep groans as he contemplated the scene.

Just as the moujik had finished performing on the *batouchka's* wife, the woman arrived with the brandy, and drinking recommenced. At last the visitor took leave and returned home; the peasant went to bed with his wife; and the false beggar lay on a bench and pretended to go to sleep, but he was only waiting for a favorable opportunity to slip away. The peasant, seeing this, purposely pretended to snore loudly, then the *pope* rose gently, and made off as fast as he could. It was with difficulty that he could reach home and open the door. As soon as he had entered the house, he slipped out of his rags, and lay down by the side of his wife. She passed her hand over his face, and, surprised to find no beard, asked; " Who has shaved you like this, *batouchka*? " — " The same devil that rogered you, " he replied. The *popadia* bit her tongue when she heard this.

LXV

The cunning woman.

A citizen had a very pretty wife. They were very poor and one day the wife said to her husband: " We must do something in order to procure food. " — " But what are we to do? " — " I have an idea but don't abuse me if I tell you. " — " No, do what you like. " — " Hide yourself, " replied his wife, "but be on the watch. I will go and find someone and bring him here; then do you knock at the door, and we will settle his business. " — " Very well. " She took a box, filled it with soot and placed it in the loft. The husband concealed himself; the wife painted and dressed herself, then left the house and went and sat under the window. Soon afterwards the *pope* passed on horseback; he came up to the pretty woman and said: " Why are you dressed in this way, young woman? Is it a feast day with you?" — " No, it is no feast. I dressed myself in this way to amuse myself; I am alone in the house. " — " And your husband, where is he? " — " He is out at work. " — " Well, my dear, I can solace you in your distress; let me step in and you shall not pass the night alone. " — " You are welcome, *batouchka.* " — " But what shall I do with my horse? "

Lead it into the courtyard, and I will send the man to put it in the stable. "

They entered the *izba*. —" In the first place, my dear, " said the *pope*, " we must drink; — here is a ruble; send for some spirits. " — The serving-man fetched them a bottle of vodka, which they drank, and ate some dainties. " Now, " said the *pope*, " It is time to go to bed; let us get between the sheet and cuddle. " —" Listen, *batouchka*! As at any rate we shall commit a sin, be quite naked, that will be more pleasant. "

The *pope* completely undressed himself, but just at the moment that he was getting into bed, a violent knock was heard at the door.

" Oh, woe is me! My husband has returned! Get up into the loft, *batouchka* and hide yourself in the chest. " — Without stopping to dress himself, the priest followed this advice, and lay down in the soot. The husband entered the room grumbling. " Why were you so long in opening the door, you bitch? " —He went up to the table, drank a glass of spirits, and ate a morsel of meat, then left the house and hid himself again. The wife returned to her former place window.

The deacon chanced to pass and the same comedy was enacted with him. When the husband knocked at the door, the deacon, quite naked, jumped into the box of soot, and fell on the top of the priest. " Who is there? " — " It is I, " replied the *pope* in a low voice, " And who are you, my friend? " — " I am the deacon, *batouchka*. " —" But how is it you are here? " — " And you, *batouchka*, by what chance are you here? " — " Be quiet or the master of the house will hear us, and it will be the worse for us. "

The woman next caught the clerk in the same manner and he in his turn joined the *pope* and the deacon in the soot box. " Who is there? " he asked. " It is I and the deacon, " replied the *pope*, " And it seems to me you are the clerk. " — " That is so, *batouchka*. "

The young woman again returned into the street, and brought in the sexton. As soon as he had undressed, a violent knocking was heard at the door and he quickly jumped into the chest. " Who is there? " — " It is I, my son, with the father, deacon, and the clerk; and you, are you not the sexton? " — " Truly I am, *batouchka*! " — " Ah well, now my friend, the clerical staff of the parish is complete. "

The husband entered, and said to his wife: " Have we not some soot to sell? Someone wants to buy some. " — " Sell it then, " she replied, " There is a chest full in the loft. " — With the help of the serving man, the husband brought down the chest, put it on a cart, and drove off. On the road, he met the carriage of a *barine*. " Stand on one side! " cried the *barine*, as loudly as he could. — " I can't; I have devils

in my cart. " — " Ah! show them to me! " said
the *barine*. — " Give me five-hundred rubles. "
— " Why do you ask such a sum? " — " Because if I open the chest to show you them, they
will all bolt out at once. " — The *barine* gave
the five-hundred rubles, but as soon as the
peasant opened the chest all the clericals of the
parish, black as real devils, jumped out and
ran away with all speed.

ANOTHER VERSION

A *moujik* had a young and pretty wife. The *pope*, the deacon and the clerk, were all in love with her. " Well, *matouchka*, " said the *pope* to her, " Is it not possible to? —" " Come this evening, *batouchka*; as soon as it is dark. " — To the deacon who made the same request, she replied: " Come, father deacon, when it is quite dark. " —To the clerk she gave a rendezvous at midnight. The *moujik*, who knew all about the affair, left home, taking a number of sacks with him, as though he were going to market. The *pope* came to see the woman, but he had hardly undressed himself, before there was a knock at the door; the husband had returned. The *pope* hid himself in a large chest. Then came the deacon, and he sought refuge in the same hiding place, and fell on the top of the *pope* and after them came the clerk, who also hid in the chest and fell on the top of the deacon. —" Wife, " cried the *moujik*, " Give me my gun, I am going to practise; chalk me out a target on that old chest. " —The woman began to do so. —" Put it higher! " whispered the *pope*. " Mark it low down! " begged the clerk. — After he had well frightened them, the peasant ordered his wife to set them at liberty, but he stood on the door-sill with a thick cudgel and gave them a good thrashing as they all ran out.

The clerk and the deacon ran home; as to the *pope* he hid himself in the stable under the cow. The peasant saw it, and said to his wife, " Go and fetch the *popadia;* she has long wanted to

buy the cow and now I will sell it to her cheaply. " — On hearing this, the *popadia* left her bed, dressed herself, and ran to the peasant's house. " Well, Ivan, will you sell me your cow? " — " Yes, *matouchka.* " — " How much do

you ask? " — " Forty rubles; but if you will
let me take my pleasure with you, I will give
you the cow for nothing. " — " I agree to that. "
— The peasant laid down the *popadia* and futtered her, then he said, " I will send the cow and
the calf tomorrow, *matouchka*. " — The *popadia* went home. " Give me some supper, " then
cried the peasant to his wife. — " What would
you like? " —" Give me some milk. " —" There
is none; the calf has drunk it all. " — The
peasant took his cudgel and gave the *pope* a
thrashing. The *pope* at first cried like a calf,
but at last he could bear it no longer and rushed
out of the house and ran home. — " Where have
you been? " asked his wife, " You come home
after midnight; you are always going after
somewhere! " — " Hold your tongue, you
bitch! " replied the *pope*, " Where is the cow
you bought? "

ANOTHER VERSION

A blacksmith had a wife who was very beautiful. They were very poor. One day the husband
said to his spouse, " Listen, wife! What are
we to do? Where shall we get some money?
You can pick up a lover, you are pretty
enough to turn the head of a rich man, go out
in the street and perhaps you will meet some
fool. But mind what you are about, if anyone

solicits your favors, first insist on the money in advance and then tell him to come to the forge at night and enter by the chimney. I will be there and arrange matters for him. " — The wife dressed herself up and went out.

The first person who spoke to her was the *pope* who knew her. — " Good day, little woman! Is your husband at home? " — " No, *batouchka!* The *barine* has sent for him and he will be at work there for a month, so now I am alone. " — " Ah, my dear, if you are alone it is so much the better. Can I come and pass the night with you? " — " Why not, *batouchka*? Only give me twenty rubles. " — " So be it, my dear, here they are. I will come to you this evening, soon after vespers. " — " Very well, *batouchka*, but do not come to the *izba*; I shall pass the night at the forge in order to watch over my husband's tools; you can see me there on the quiet. Come down the chimney. " — " All right, my dear. " — Having received the *pope's* money she continued her walk.

The churchwarden met her. " Ah, good day *kouznetchikha!* (1) " — " Good day, good man. " —" Is your husband at home? " — " No, he has gone to the *barine's* house and will be at work there for a month, so that now I am alone in the house. " " Cannot I spend a night with you,

(1) A blacksmith's wife.

my dear? " — " Why not? At present I am free,
give me twenty rubles and come tonight rather
late; I shall sleep in the forge, but when you
come, make no noise and instead of knocking
at the door, slip quietly down the chimney. " —
" That's agreed! " — She took the churchwarden's twenty rubles, and continued her walk.

A *Tsigane* met her and said: " Good day my
charmer! " — " Good day, *Tsigane!* " — " Is
your old man at home, my well-beloved? " —
" No, he has gone to the *barine*'s to work, and
will be away a month, so now I am alone. " —
" Ah, my beauty! Then I can pass the night
with you? " — " Certainly you can come, but
give me twenty rubles, *Tsigane*. " — The *Tsigane* pulled the money out of his pocket. " Here
you are, my pretty one! Tonight I will come to
you. " — " Come to the forge, *Tsigane*, and de-
scend the chimney, I will await you there. " —
" Very well, my dove. "

The *kouznetchikha* returned home and said
to her husband. " Well, little man, tonight I
shall receive the visit of three lovers; I have
taken twenty rubles from each of them. " —
" All right, wife. God be praised! I will settle
their business for them. "

As soon as it was dark, the *moujik* went to the
forge, lighted a fire, made his pincers hot, and
awaited the lovers. The *pope* hurried through the
vespers as fast as possible, put on his cassock,

and ran straight from the church to the forge. On the road he met the church-warden. " Where are you going, *batouchka*? " " Be silent about it, my friend, but I have sinned against God, and am going to pass the night with the blacksmith's wife and I have paid in advance. " — " That doesn't matter, my friend. We will go together; that will be more amusing. " — Just as they were approaching the forge, the *Tsigane* joined them. " Ah, holy fathers, where are you going? " — " Be quiet, *Tsigane*; we are going to pass the night with a woman, in that forge you see there. " — " Ah, holy fathers, I also am going to see her. " —" Very well, come with us. "

The three men came to the forge. " Now who is to be the first to go down the chimney? " — " I, my friends, " replied the *pope*, " I am the eldest. " — " Very well; go on, *batouchka*. " — The priest took off his cassock, his boots and his socks; the church-warden and the *Tsigane* fastened cords under his arms, and then prepared to lower him down the chimney. " My friends, " said the *pope* to them, " As soon as I have finished my business, I will cry, *Fuik*! You will reply: *Shmuik*! and then you will pull me up. "

No sooner had the *pope* made his descent, then the blacksmith seized with his red hot pincers the genital parts of the *batouchka*. " *Fuik!* " cried the priest in desperation. " *Shmuik*, " replied his companions, and pulled him up. " You finished very quickly, *batouchka*, " remarked the *Tsigane*. — " Ah, my friend, what a hot hole she has. I had no sooner touched it than I was burned as though by a flash of gunpowder. I have never met anything like it. " — " Now then it is my turn, " said the church-warden. " Go on. " — The church-warden undressed himself, and the *pope* and the *Tsigane* passed a cord under his arms and lowered him into the forge, where he was received by the husband in the same way as his predecessor had been. " *Fuik* " he cried. " *Shmuik*, " said the others, and they hauled him out of the chimney. " Well, *Tsigane*, " said the church-warden, when he was at the top, " I do not regret my twenty rubles. It was worth it. It is your turn now. " — " I shall not be like you, holy fathers. I shall not leave her till I have performed three times. So listen to what I say, holy fathers. Do not pull me up till you have heard me cry out *Fuik* three times. " — " Very good. "

The *Tsigane* was lowered. As soon as the blacksmith found that the third lover was in the chimney, his hot pincers again did their work. " *Fuik* " cried the *Tsigane* at the top of his voice, but no one appeared to hear him. " *Fuik*, " he cried again, but the second appeal remained without a response. " *Fuik*, " a third time shouted the poor wretch. " Damn you, *batouchka*. There is no rogering here, but they burn you alive instead *Fuik!* " — " *Shmuik!* " replied the *pope* and the church-warden, pulling up the cord. As soon as he was out of the forge, the *Tsigane,* whose testicles were in a sad state, began to violently abuse the *pope.* " Old goat-beard. Why did you not say how you had been received down there? May the devil take you. You alone ought to have had your testicles burned. Oh, holy fathers, he has scorched me worse than either of you. " —" That is nothing, my friend. The whore has deceived us, let us all go to the *izba* and settle accounts with her. "

They put on their clothes the best way they could, and hobbled along till they came to the house of the blacksmith, and there they found the woman at home. " How have you treated us, you wretched woman? " — " Ah, my dear friends, " she replied, " I am deeply grieved that the devil moved my husband to come home. He returned unexpectedly, and this evening went to work at the forge. Sit down, friends, while I dress myself. We have all the night before us: my husband is now at the smithy, and will remain there till the morning. "

The visitors sat down. Suddenly they heard the blacksmith arrive. He pretended to be drunk, knocked loudly at the door, and abused his wife. " Open the door, you whore. " On hearing this noise, and these shouts, the three men

rose hurridely. " What will become of us now? "
— " Don't be afraid, friends, " said the *kouznet-chikha*. " I will conceal you. He is drunk and will soon go to sleep. You, *batouchka*, quickly take off all your clothes, and stand quite naked in that corner. I will tell my husband that I have bought an idol. "

The *pope* pulled off his cassock, boots, socks, and shirt and placed himself in the place indicated in the position of an idol, which his white beard and scanty hair made him resemble. " And I? — where shall I put myself? " asked the church-warden. — " And I? " said the *Tsigane*. — " You, my friends, undress yourselves completely. You, " — she said addressing the church-warden — " I will fasten by a rope to this hook, and I will tell my husband that I have bought a large cask. As for you, *Tsigane*, you get into that mash-tub and keep quiet, and he will not even see you. "

They both stripped and the mistress of the house fastened the church-warden to the hook with a rope, and the *Tsigane* jumped into the mash-tub. Then the *kouznetchikha* opened the door to her husband. He came in grumbling, and cried: " Wife, give me some supper! " Then he looked around, and saw the *pope* standing in the corner. " Ah, what is that big devil over there? "
— " May the Lord help you! That a devil! It is an idol! " — " How much did you pay for

such a big one? — " I will tell you tomorrow; now go to bed. " The blacksmith lighted a candle, walked up to the *pope* and laid hold of his member. " What is this for? " asked the blacksmith of his wife. — " To put a candle in. " " Very good! I will put one in. " He took the candle, and placed it on that part of the *pope's* person, but the candle fell off and rolled on the ground. " If this candlestick is made red hot it will hold the candle better. " So saying the blacksmith applied the flame of the candle to the tip of the priest's yard. The *pope* unable to stand the pain, jumped over the table, and, naked though he was, ran out of the *izba.* " Ah, you whore! " cried the husband, " That is not an idol you have bought, but a devil. You see he has run away, and you have lost your money. "

He then drew near the hook. " But what is this hanging here? " —" It is a big cask that I have bought to hold water. " — " What? a cask? It is a fine tub, but is it sound? " — " Yes; I struck it with my fist and it rang well. " — " Wait a bit! I will try it with a thick stick and we shall see if it does not break. " He took a cudgel and belabored with all his might the ribs of the church-warden, who swung backwards and forwards like a pendulum. At last the rope broke, the church-warden cracked his head against the floor, but jumped up with a bound and quickly gained the door. " Well, you have made some fine bargains, " remarked the blacksmith. " Now I am going to drink some kvass. "

He walked up to the tub, and saw the *Tsigane* up to his neck in the mash, with only his head uncovered. The blacksmith crossed himself. "This is the result of living with a slut like you. You must have kept these grains in the tub ever since you married me and the devils have bred in it. " He nailed a lid on the top of the tub, and the poor *Tsigane* remained there two days without any food.

On the third day, the blacksmith harnessed his horse, put the tub into the cart, and drove to the lake. When he arrived there, he took off his boots, tucked up his trousers and waded into the lake. Then he walked along in the water holding his whip as though he had been fishing. In a little time a *barine* passed that way. " Good day, *moujik*, " — " Ah, *barine*, why did you speak to me? You have spoiled my fishing. " " What do you mean by spoiled my fishing? " — " Yes, a devil was just on the point of nibbling at my hook, and now you have scared it away. " — " What absurd tales you are telling me. " — " What do you mean by tales? I had already caught one and put him in that tub and I should have caught another if you had not frightened him. " —" Show me the one you have caught! " — " I will not show it, *barine* " — " Here are

fifty rubles for you. " — " Up at home, my
masters would give me a hundred. " —" Very
well, I will give you a hundred rubles. " The
blacksmith took the *barine's* money and opened
the tub; the *Tsigane* immediately jumped out, all
covered with grains from head to foot, and ran
away as fast as his legs could carry him. " Truly
it is a devil, " said the *barine* and spat. " It is
the first time I have ever seen one in all my life. "

When he returned home, the blacksmith said to
his wife: " Well, wife, I have sold the *Tsigane*
for a hundred rubles; now there only remains to
sell the *pope's* cassock and we shall have done

an excellent stroke of business. " He put on the
cassock, took the *batouchka's* cane, and went
early in the morning to the priest's house. The
pope, when he saw the blacksmith, said to himself: " It will be a bad business for me if my
parishioners should hear of my adventure. " —
So he begged of his visitor to conceal the affair.
" I beg of you, friend, not to let the people laugh
at my expense. " —" What will you give me?
Will you buy back these articles for a hundred
rubles? " — " It is not a hundred rubles that
I offer you but a hundred-and-fifty. " — On
receiving the money, the blacksmith returned
to the *pope* the cassock and the cane. Then he
returned home, and from that time the couple
lived a little more comfortably.

LXVI

The Jewess.

A lad went to seek for work; on the road he
entered an inn to pass the night. The inn was
kept by a Jew and his wife. When evening came
they all lay on the floor. In the night the Jewess
was too warm and whilst half asleep and half
awake she threw off all she had on her, and lay
with her arse uncovered. At this sight the lad
was seized with a desire, which he unhesitating-

ly gratified; he attacked his host's wife and began to roger her. " Volko! Volko! " said the Jewess, thinking it was her husband. " Be quiet with your Volko, " replied the lad, " Or you will

awaken the Jew. " — The woman passed her hand over the head of the young man and did not find there the curls which the Jews are accustomed to wear. " Volko, is that you? " she asked. " Be silent. " said the lad, and made haste to finish his business.

LXVII

Nicholas the hermit.

An old peasant had a young wife. She often received the visits of a young man who was in love with her and who was named Terekha Gladkoi. The old man found it out and said to his spouse: " Wife, I went to the wood and found Nicholas the hermit, whatever you ask him he will grant. " The next morning he went off to the forest, found an old pine-tree, and sat himself in the hollow trunk. His wife set to work, and after she had made a goodly number of pies and little rolls, and savoury *blines*, and went to the wood to pray to Nicholas the hermit.

When she came near the pine-tree she saw the old man. " There is Nicholas the hermit, " she said to herself, and she began to pray: " *Ba-touchka* Nicholas, cause my husband to become blind! " — " Return home, woman, " replied the old man, " your husband shall lose his sight; but leave your pies here. " The peasant woman put down the basket at the foot of the tree and returned home. Soon afterwards the old man left his hiding place, ate up the pies, the rolls, and the *blines*; then he cut himself a thick stick, and made his way to his house. When he neared home he began to grope with his hands and tap with his stick like a blind man. " Why are you walking so carefully, old man? " asked his wife. " Cannot you see well? " — " Alas, my darling, a misfortune has happened to me, and I have lost my sight. " The woman took her husband by the arm led him into the house, and made him sit down by the stove.

On the evening of the same day she received a visit from her lover, Terekha Gladkoi. " Now you need no longer be afraid, " she said, " Come and see me whenever you like. Today I went to the wood and I prayed to Nicholas the hermit to make my husband blind, and he has just come back to the house and cannot see at all. " — Then the young woman made some *blines*, and when they were put on the table, Terekha began to eat them greedily. " Take care, Terekha, not to choke yourself with the *blines*, " said the woman, " I will bring you something to moisten them. She went to fetch some butter and as soon as she was gone, the old man took a cross-bow, loaded it, aimed, and shot Terekha Gladkoi dead. Then he jumped off the stove, rolled up a *bline* into a ball and stuffed it into Terekha's mouth that it might look as though he had choked himself, and having done that he resumed his place on the stove.

The woman returned with the butter, and seeing Terekha lifeless, she cried, " I told you not to eat *blines* without butter or you would choke yourself. You would not listen to me and now you are dead! " —She took the body of the young man, dragged it under the staircase, and went to bed. As she could not sleep alone, she called to her husband to come to her, but he replied, " I am very well where I am. " After some time he cried as though he were in a dream, " Wife, get up! Terekha Gladkoi is lying dead under our staircase. " — " Did you see that in a dream, old man? " she asked.

The husband came down from the stove, pushed the body of Terekha Gladkoi out of the house, and dragged it to the residence of a rich *moujik*. Before the door was a cask of honey; the old man placed the body against it and put in the dead man's hand a scoop, so that Terekha had the appearance of being engaged in taking the honey out of the cask. The *moujik* saw him and took him for a thief, so he ran up and gave him a blow on the head with a cudgel. The body, of course, rolled on the ground, and the old man, who had hidden himself in a corner, quickly ran up and collared the *moujik*, " Why have you killed this young man? " — " I will give you a hundred rubles if you will not say a word about it to any one replied the *moujik*. " — " Give me five hundred, or I will deliver you up to justice. " The *moujik* gave the five-hundred rubles.

The old man took the body and dragged it to the *pope's* house. Then he took a horse out of the *pope's* stable, put Terekha on its back, and let the animal loose. The *pope* rushed out, began to curse Terekha, and tried to stop him; the horse galloped into the stable and the rider came into collision with a beam of wood, was thrown out of the saddle, and rolled on the ground at the horse's feet. Then the old man came up and seized the *pope* by the beard. " Why have you killed this young man? Come with me to the police! "

What was to be done? The *pope* gave the old man three-hundred rubles, on condition that he would hold his tongue, and proceeded to bury the defunct.

ANOTHER VERSION

A *pope* had a wife who deceived him and had a lover. The *pope's* man-servant discovered this intrigue, and did all he could to oppose it. " How can I get rid of him? " said the faithless spouse to herself, and she went to ask the advice of an old witch, but the man-servant had long before made arrangements with her. " My dear friend, " said the erring wife; " Help me to get rid of the *pope* and his man-servant. " — " Go to the wood, " replied the old woman " and there you will find Nicholas the hermit. Address yourself to him, and he will help you. "

The *pope's* wife went the wood and sought for Nicholas the hermit. The man-servant had thoroughly disguised himself, and floured his beard, and hidden himself in a hollow-tree. He uttered a groan which attracted the attention of the young woman: she turned her eyes in the direction from whence it came, and saw inside a hollow-tree, an old man with white hair. She approached the tree. " *Batouchka* Nicholas the hermit, " she said, "how can I kill the *pope* and his servant? " — " Oh, woman, woman! " replied Nicholas the hermit, " To kill them would be a crime, but I can deprive them of sight. Tomorrow make a great number of *blines* with butter and they will eat them and become blind:

if also you cook some eggs they will lose their hearing after they have eaten. "

When she returned home the woman prepared the *blines*, and the next day she baked them and cooked some eggs. The *pope* and his servant were about to start off to work in the country, and she invited them to breakfast before they started. Then she served the *blines* and the eggs and spared nothing. " Eat these with plenty of butter, my dear friends, " she said, " that will be nicer. " The servant had told the *pope* what to do. When they had eaten, they began to say: " How dark it is! " and groped their way to the wall. " What is the matter, my friends? " — " God has punished us, we cannot see. " — The woman helped them to lie down on the stove, after which she called her lover, and they began to drink and to play. " Let me f..k you," said the lover, " but from behind, like the goats do. " The young woman put herself in the required position, and her lover mounted on her. Then the *pope* and the servant jumped off the stove and fell on the guilty couple.

LXVIII

The two brothers.

A peasant had two sons, both of an age to settle down in life. The old man consulted his wife on this

subject. " Which of our two sons shall marry ? "
he asked the old woman; " Gritza or Laur? "
— " Let the eldest marry, " she replied. And
during the carnival, they betrothed Laur to a
young girl of a neighbouring village. Holy week
came and then Lent being finished, Laur prepared to pay a visit to his future wife in company with his brother Gritzka. They rode in a carriage drawn by two horses, and Laur as the fiance occupied the master's place, whilst his brother acted
as coachman.

They had hardly quitted the village than Laur,
who had made up for his long abstinence in Lent,
required to let down his trousers. " Brother
Gritzka, " he said, " stop the horses. " —" Why? "
— " I want to ease myself. " —" What a fool
you are? You can't do that on our land. Wait a
bit and we shall cross a neighbor's field, and
there you can deposit all you have in your belly. "
— Laur was obliged to wait, with the sweat
rolling down his face.

Soon the carriage entered a neighbor's field.
" Now, brother, " said Laur, " Be kind enough
to stop the horses. I cannot hold out any longer:
it is more than I can bear. " — " You are a
fool, " replied Gritzka. " Why did you not
speak whilst we were passing through our own
fields? There, you could have done as you liked.
But now the case is different, and you know
well enough that it is not proper to deposit filth

J. Wely
95

in another man's field. Besides, some devil
might see us, and beat us both, and take away
our horses. Hold in a bit; when we arrive
in your father-in-law's court-yard, jump out
of the carriage and go straight to the privy.
There you can relieve yourself, and I meanwhile will unharness the horses. " — Laur remained in the carriage and bore his discomfort
as best he could.

They arrived in the village, and entered the
father-in-law's court-yard. Near the gate stood
the mother of the future bride, who welcomed
her future son-in-law with the words, " Good day,
my son, my dearest! We have been waiting
for you a long time already. " Without answer-
ing a word, Laur jumped out, and made his
way towards the privy. Thinking that he was
timid, the old woman seized him by the arm,
and said: " Why are you ashamed, my son?
May God be with you. Do not be afraid; there
is no stranger with us, and I humbly beg you to
enter the house. " She led him at once into the
izba, and made him sit at the top of the table.
Being no longer able to contain himself, Laur let
fly in his trousers, and sat motionless in his place,
being afraid to make the least movement. The
mistress of the house meantime hurried about,
and prepared a repast for her guests, then took
a decanter of brandy, and filled a glass which
she handed to the fiance. He rose to take it, but

at that moment the fecal matter in the seat of his pantaloons slipped down his thighs decended into his boots and infected all the *izba*. " Where does this stink come from? " The mother-in-law searched in every corner to see if the children had not made a mess somewhere. No! She could not find a trace of anything, so the old woman then addressed her visitors. " My friends, our courtyard is very dirty; one of you has perhaps put his foot in some dirty mess. " She first went to Gritzka, and not finding upon him what she sought, she approached Laur. " Ah, son-in-law, you no sooner came into the yard than you turned towards the privy; have you besh...t yourself? " She began to feel the young man's clothes, and on touching his knees, she dirtied her hand.

Then she began to abuse Laur. " You must have lost your senses! What the devil is the matter with you? It was certainly to make game of us, and not to pay us a friendly visit that you came here, you rascal. He has eaten and drunk nothing in the house, and he already makes a mess under him at the table. Go to the devil, and be his son-in-law and not ours. " — Thereupon the old woman called her daughter, and said: " My dear child, I will not allow you to marry this dirty beast. Marry his brother; he is the right man for you! " Laur was pushed on one side, and his place was given to Gritzka; then the repast commenced and the company ate and drank till evening.

When night came, all went to bed. The mistress of the house said to the visitors: " You will sleep in the new *izba*. You, daughter, prepare a bed for your future husband. As for this dirty blackguard, there is no need to prepare one for him; he can sleep on a bench. " The two young men went to bed; but whilst Gritzka had a feather bed, Laur was obliged to lie on a bench; he could not sleep and thought only of the best way to revenge himself for the trick his brother had played him. When he heard Gritzka snoring, he rose, and gently pushed the table against the door, after which he lay down again on his bench.

At midnight Gritzka awoke; he quitted his bed and wanted to relieve himself. He tried to leave the house, but when he went towards where he thought the door was, he knocked against the table. " What is the meaning of this? Where is the door? " he asked himself. He retraced his steps, and groped about but though he felt everywhere he only encountered the walls. " What can have become of the door? " However his necessity became pressing, and tormented him more and more. What was to be done? Gritzka sat down near the table and discharged the load which inconvenienced him. Then he reflected. " This is a bad job; I must get rid of this between now and to-morrow morning. " On looking around he saw a large crack in the wall, and thought he would put his misdeed out of sight, but he missed his aim, and the fecal matter struck the wall by the side of the crack and rebounded into his face. Gritzka wiped himself with his hands, and then took a double handful, and made a fresh attempt, but with no more success than on the first occasion. He only succeeded in dirtying the wall, and dirtying himself. He must wash himself, and so the poor young man began to search for some water. By feeling about he discovered on the stove a saucepan which contained some dye, which had been used for coloring the Easter eggs. He took the saucepan off the stove, and washed his face and hands. " Now, the misfortune is rectified; " and with this reflection Gritzka went to bed again. As soon as he was asleep, his brother arose noiselessly, and put the table back in its proper place.

It was broad daylight when the girl woke up her sweetheart. " Get up, dearest, " she said, " breakfast is ready. " But what was her fright, when casting her eyes on her future husband, she saw that he looked like a devil. The girl was frightened and fled, and ran weeping to her mother. " Why are you weeping? " asked the old woman. " Why should I not weep? Come and see for yourself what has hap-

pened in the new *izba*! " —" But what can have
happened there? Your fiance is there with his
brother. " — " What do you mean by my fiance?
It is a devil and not a man! " — All three, the
father, the mother and the young girl, went to
the *izba* where the future husband had passed the
night. On seeing them, Gritzka put on a joyous
smile; his teeth only were white but all the rest of
his face was a dark blue which gave him the appearance of a veritable demon.

The master and mistress of the house fled.
The old man carefully closed the door of the
izba and went to the *pope*. " *Batouchka*, come
and bless our new *izba* and drive out the impure
spirit; the devil one has taken possession of it! "
— " What, my friend, there are devils in your
house? But I also am afraid of devils, friend! "
—" Don't be afraid, *batouchka*! I have a mare!
If anything should happen, spur it up and gallop
away, there is not a devil or even a bird that
could catch you. " —" Very well, friend, I will
drive away the impure spirit, only the mare must
belong to me. " — " It shall be yours, *batouchka*;
it shall be yours, " replied the *moujik* bowing
before the priest.

The priest went to the *izba* accompanied by a
deacon and a sacristan; they were clad in their
sacerdotal garments, and each held in his hand a
censer in which burned a few grains of incense.
The three men marched round the *izba* singing.

" Oh, Lord most holy ! " — " Ah, " thought Gritzka, " here is the *pope* with his cross. I will stand near the door and when he comes in, I will ask his blessing. " He placed himself near the door and waited. After he had made the circuit of the *izba* three times, the *pope* was about to enter, but as soon as he crossed the threshold he drew back hurriedly, for Gritzka was standing there with a blue hand outstretched. The priest fled at once, jumped on the mare's back, and having no whip, beat the horses flanks with the censer. The animal started off at a gallop; the *pope* tried to pull up the horse, but only made it go all the faster. In its headlong flight the mare ran up against an obstacle. The *pope* lost his seat, was thrown, and cracked his skull. As to the two brothers, they returned home, neither having succeeded better than the other.

LXIX

The girl without a head.

A peasant lived with his wife. He took a cow to the fair, and sold it to a *moujik* from another village; after they had drunk a bottle of wine together the two men began to fraternise. " Well mate, now we are friends for ever. " " Certainly, mate, why not? " After that, every time they

met they looked on each other as an old friend,
and had a friendly glass together. One day by
chance they met in an eating house. " Ah, good
day, mate. " —" Good day mate! How is your
cow ? " — " Thank God
she is all right. " — " So
much the better; praise be
to God ! But look here,
mate : cannot we unite our
families " — " Why not ?
You have a son of an age
to set up for himself, and I
have a daughter to marry. "
— " Very good, then we
may look upon that as
being settled, eh? "—" Certainly; that is arranged. "
They talked together for a
few minutes, and then
parted, when he returned
home, the peasant who had
sold the cow, said to his
son: " Thanks to me, my
boy, you can get married.
I have found a wife for you. " —" Where did you
find her, father? " " Do you remember my mate,
to whom I sold a cow lately? " — " Yes, father. "
— " Well, my mate has a daughter — a beauty. "
—" Have you seen her? " —" No; but her father told me so. " —" If you have not seen her

you cannot brag about her beauty. You know well enough one should never buy a pig in a poke. Let me go to their village and I will find out what sort of a girl she is. " —" Very good, go, and God be with you. "

The young man dressed himself as poorly as he could, put a bridle over his shoulder, took a whip in his hand, and went off to the house of his father's friend. He arrived in the evening and knocked at the window of the *izba*. " Good day, master. " —" Good day, my man, " replied the master of the house, " What is it you want? " — " Give me shelter for the night! " — " Where do you come from? " — " From far off; I live a hundred *versts* from here. I am looking for my master's horses, *diadouchka*; they were stolen from me at a place where I had stopped for the night, and for three days I have been looking for them, and cannot find them. " " Very well, stop with us. "

The young man entered the house, took the bridle off his shoulder, and hung it on a nail; then he sat on a bench and began to examine the young girl. " And what good news is there with you? " asked the peasant of his guest. — " The news with us is not good, *diadouchka*; we hear of nothing but misfortune. " — " What is that? " —" Why, every night there are people eaten by wolves; for the last fortnight there has hardly been a night when the wolves did not de-

vour five or even ten persons. " The conversation
was continued for some time, and then all went
to bed; the old man and his wife in the chamber;
their daughter and the traveller in the vestibule;
but the former in a bed, and the latter on a heap
of hay.

When he laid down the lad listened for a long
while, expecting that the young girl would receive
a visit from some lover. One hour, two hours
passed, and then a knock was heard at the door.
" Open, dearest, " said a voice. The girl rose
noiselessly, opened the door, and her lover entered, he undressed himself and got into bed
with her. After they had talked a bit, the visitor
got on the girl and rode her twice. " Listen,
dearest: Women have told me that if the legs
are tied to the neck with a cord the slit is stretched open, and it is very good it appears to futter
that way; there is hardly a movement to make. "
— " Let us try it, dearest. " The lover did not
need to be asked twice; with his belt he fastened
the girl's legs up to her neck, and began to roger
her in that position.

The traveller, who lay in the vestibule, then
quickly rose to his feet, and cried with all his
might. " Look out! Get up master! You have
lost your daughter: The wolves have eaten her
head. " The lover made to the door in one bound,
but the traveller seized him by the collar. " No,
my friend: You will stop here! Wait a minute. "

On hearing the cries of their guest, the peasant and his wife ran hurriedly out of their room, and came to their daughter's bed. The old man felt in the bed in the dark, and his hand encountered a coynte and an arse; he was greatly frightened, and thought it was only a trunk without any head. " Bring a light quickly! We have lost our child! " he cried to his wife, and began to weep over his daughter whose coynte and arse he still held in his hand.

The old woman returned with a candle. " Look she is tied up! Oh! Lord, what is the meaning of this. " — " Here is the wolf, *diadouchka*, " said the traveller bringing forward his prisoner. " Oh, son of a bitch that you are! " cried the mother. " Couldn't you futter her simply and fairly? " The gallant was taken by the shoulders, and pushed out of the house, and the girl was untied. " I beg of you, friend, " said the old man to his guest, " not to speak of our misfortune to anyone, here are twenty-five rubles for you to purchase your silence. " —" No, *diadouchka* I will not mention it. May God help you; — it is no business of mine! "

The next morning, the peasant gave the young man a good breakfast, and escorted him to the end of the village. On his road home, the young man met a band of beggars, each with his wallet.

"Listen to me, poor people, " said he, " Go to

such and such a place at the far end of this village; a rich peasant lives there, who is celebrating a service for his daughter, who had her head
eaten by wolves. He is a good man, he will receive you and give you something to eat and
even put something in your wallets. " The beggars went straightway to the indicated address.
When they arrived in the court-yard of the peasant's house, they stood in a row and waited for
their dinner. " What a lot there are of them, "
said the peasant, when he perceived them. He
took a large round loaf and cut off a slice for each
of the beggars; but when the distribution was
finished, they still did not move. " What are you
waiting for? " asked the *moujik.* " I have given
you alms. " — " But, *diadouchka,* it would be
but kind to give us a dinner in memory of your
daughter. " — " What daughter? " " Why the
one the wolves have eaten. " — " Who the devil
told you that? Nothing of the kind has happened
at my house. " — " We were told by a young
man, who sent us here. " — " Get out! De-
camp! " roared the peasant.

The beggars went away, and the *moujik* said
to his wife: " Well, old woman, I have made a
nice mess of it. The money that I gave to that son
of a bitch was a dead loss; he promised not to
tell anyone, and he had hardly left here than he
sent us a whole band of beggars. He must certainly have told the story throughout the coun-

try side. If my mate should hear of it, the marriage would be spoiled. "

During this time the young man continued his journey. When he arrived home, his parents said to him: " Well, my son, have you seen your future wife? " — " Ah, father, don't renew my grief; it would have been better if I had never seen her. " — " Why so? " — " She whom you destined for my wife (God rest her soul) has had her head devoured by wolves; — only the trunk was left. They are going to bury her to-morrow. " " What a misfortune for that poor family! We must go, old woman, and see the poor girl before they bury her. Those people have been very kind to us! Harness the horse, son; your mother and I will go and see our old friend. "

The young man harnessed the horse, the two old people mounted the car and started off. When the vehicle drew near the house, the peasant saw his friends, and ran out to meet them. " Good day, mate: how are you? Come into the *izba*, my dear visitors! " — " Thank you, mate," they replied sadly, " but we are not making a visit; we have come to pay the last farewell to your daughter. Evidently it was decreed that there was not to be an alliance between our two families. " — " Why not, mate. " — " Why, there has been a sad accident in your house; the wolves have eaten up your daughter. " — " When?

Who told you that? " — " It was my son; he
lodged at your house last night, and saw the accident with his own eyes. " — " Oh, indeed! That is
curious! So that was your son! Well, there's
nothing to be said; for though my daughter is
still alive, the match is broken off. " After a
little conversation they separated and from that
day, the two peasants ceased to call each other
" mate. "

ANOTHER VERSION

A soldier who was on furlough received hospitality for a night at the house of a *pope*. This
pope had a daughter of whom the soldier had
heard talk on the road; it was said that she had
intimate relations with a young man. Supper
was served, and the master and mistress of the
house sat down with their guest. " Where do you
serve, soldier? " asked the *pope*. — " At Piter (1),
batouchka. " — " Do you often see the
Czar? " — " Continually. " " Is there any news? "
— " Yes, I have heard something, — but I
must not repeat it. " — " Tell us what it is, friend. "
— " You will know, when the ukase is issued. "
— " No, tell us now, please " — " Well, " replied
the soldier, as though overcome by the pertina-
city of the priest; " It is going to be made obli-

(1) The popular name for Saint-Petersburg.

gatory on every woman when she is futtered to
have her head and feet passed through a horse-
collar. What severe laws are always being made.
Even when you lie with a woman you must observe certain rules! " — " There is nothing to
be done: The czar is master," observed the *pope*.

His daughter, who was present at this conversation, had not lost a word. When bed-time
came, she took her place on the stove, and the
soldier mounted into the loft. " Give me a thick
stick, *batouchka*, " he said to the *pope*. " Why do
you want it, soldier? " — " Why, very likely
wolves come into your house in the night. " —
The *pope* laughed and gave him a cudgel, and
said to his daughter: " They say there are no
fools at Piter; but isn't this soldier one? He
thinks that the wolves come into a man's house. "

At midnight the lover of the young girl came;
he drew near the stove upon which she was lying,
and would have lain with her, but she would not
permit it. " Bring me a horse-collar, " she said;
" The Czar has made a new law; — a soldier told
my father about it today. " — " And where
shall I find a horse-collar. " — " There is one
hung on a nail in the vestibule. " The lover
went and fetched the required article; put his
sweetheart's legs in the collar, lifted them as
high as he could, and then put her head in. Hardly had he commenced to f..k her than the
soldier jumped out of the loft, gave the lover a

violent blow on the arse with his cudgel, and
began to cry with all his might, " *Batouchka!*
the wolves!" The gallant decamped without finishing his business; the *pope* and his wife ran
towards the stove to see if the wolves were really
devouring their daughter.

The father seized the girl by her vulva, the
mother grabbed her by the arse. " Ah, poor
child, " they cried, " the wolves have eaten her
head. " Just then the soldier came with a light,
and the parents perceived that their daughter was
alive, but that she had her head and legs passed
through a horse-collar. The soldier at this sight
began to cry, " What! Has she dared to do that
without waiting for the Czar's order ? " — " Don't
say anything about it, " begged the *pope*, " and
here are a hundred rubles for you. " — The
soldier took the money, and said : " Very well!
so be it, *batouchka!* I pardon her on account of
her youth and foolishness, but if it had been you,
and you had rogered your wife in that way, you
would not have got off for less than a thousand
rubles! "

LXX

Women's mischief.

My dear little aunt! I want to ask you —"
" Well, speak, what is it you want ? " —

" I want, you know. " The aunt understood at once
what was the matter. " So be it, Ivanouchka, I
would like to do you a favor, but you do not
know what mischief a woman can make. " —
" Perhaps, aunt, I am not altogether incapable of
it myself. " — " Very well; come tonight under
our window. "

The lad was delighted and awaited the evening
with impatience, and as soon as it was dark went
into his uncle's farm-yard; but the ground was
covered with hemp-boon which crackled under
his feet. " See who is there, old man," said the
aunt to her husband. " Some one is walking
round the *izba*; is it a thief? " The uncle opened
the window, and asked : " Who is wandering
around here? " " It is I, uncle, " replied the nephew.
" What the devil has brought you here? " —
" Why, uncle, I have had a dispute with my
father. He declared that there were nine rows of
beams in your *izba* and I maintained there were
ten. So I have come to count them. " — " Has
the old devil lost his senses? " said the uncle.
" He helped me to build the house himself, and he
ought to know there are ten rows of timbers. "
—" That is so, uncle, that is so. I will go back
and spit in my father's face. "

The next day the lad said to his aunt: " Well,
aunt. Is there no method of having a turn with
you? " — " How silly you are! How could I
come to you whilst your uncle was talking to

you? But you know the place where we drive in the sheep; go there tonight and you will certainly see me. " The night came and the lad did not fail to be at the appointed place. He hid himself in a corner, and awaited his aunt. But she said to her husband. " Listen, old man! There is a noise in our farm-yard; it sounds as though some wild beast had come in. Our sheep are frightened. Can a wolf have got into our sheep-fold? "

The old man went into the farm-yard and called out. " Who is there? " — " Is it I, uncle. " —" What the devil brings you here at such an hour? " — " How can I help it, uncle? My father gives me no rest; just now we nearly came to blows. " — " Why so? " — " He said that you had nine sheep and a ram; I maintained that you had only nine sheep, because you had killed the ram. " — " Yes, you are right; I killed the ram for a christening dinner. The old devil was even present at that dinner, and helped to eat the ram ! Although he is my own brother, tomorrow, when I see him, I will spit in his face. " — " And I, although he is my own father, I will pull his beard out; he will not even let his own family sleep in peace! Good night, uncle. " — " Take care of yourself! " — During this conversation, the aunt was almost convulsed with laughter.

On the morrow, the nephew, when he met

her, said: " Oh, aunt, aunt! Are you not ashamed? I shall never be able to have you! " —
" Oh, Vania, how silly you are! Could I come
whilst your uncle was talking to you? That makes
twice you have failed; try to be more fortunate
the third time. Come tonight to our *izba* ; you
know where we sleep. You will be able to feel
me, I shall have my arse in the air. "

When the aunt got into bed with her husband,
she spoke to him as follows. " Listen to what I
have to say to you. I cannot stand it any longer.
For six years I have slept on the edge of the
bed; now let us change places. I want to be
against the wall. " —" It's all the same to me, "
replied the old man, and he lay down on the
edge. After some time, the woman again spoke.
" Eh, master! how hot it is in the *izba*. Just
look and see if the stove is closed. " So saying
she placed her hand on her husband's arse. " Ah,
you always wear drawers! That is not allowed.
Ask Loukian or Karp if they ever wear drawers
when they sleep with their wives. "

The husband felt the justness of this observation, so he took off his drawers, and went to
sleep with his arse in the air. Just after first
cock-crow, the nephew slipped into the vestibule, and put his ear to the door; silence reigned
in the *izba*. He opened the door gently, entered
the room, and began to feel round the bed. His
hand encountered an arse which he took to be

that of his aunt, and which he attacked vigorously.

The uncle, being assailed in this manner, uttered loud cries, and laid hold of the guilty member. " What is the matter, old man? " asked the aunt. " Get up quickly, and light a shaving, " said he in a loud voice. " I have caught a thief. "

The aunt jumped hurriedly out of bed, and pretending to believe that the house was on fire, ran and fetched some water and put out what fire there was in the stove. " Why are you pottering about? " — " There is no fire here. " — " Well then run quickly to the neighbor's house and ask for a light. " — " What? Go out now? It is dark, and wolves prowl about the village. " — " May the devil take you! I will go myself and fetch a light! You hold the thief, and see that he does not get away. " The uncle snatched up a lantern, opened the door, went to his neighbor's house, woke him, told him what had happened and asked for a light; during this time the aunt remained in the *izba* with the nephew. " Now, " she said, " you can do what you like with me. " He laid her on the bed, and trussed her twice; after which he slipped away quietly.

The young man having gone, the aunt began to reflect: " What shall I say to my husband when he reproaches me for having let the thief escape? " Fortunately for her, a cow had calved a little time before, and the calf was fastened to the bed. The cunning woman seized the calf's tongue, and held it tightly in her hand. When the husband returned with a light, he asked: " What are you holding there, wife? " — " I am holding what you put into my hand. " — The peasant flew into a violent rage, drew his knife, and cut off the poor animal's head. " What are you doing? " cried his wife. " Have you lost your senses? Are you mad? " He let down his drawers and showed his arse. " Look how he licked me! I don't think I should have survived another touch of his tongue. "

When the aunt next met her nephew, she said: " Vania, will you buy me some new shoes? " — " Why not? Tomorrow I shall be going to the town, and I will buy them. " —" Buy them, Vania, and I will reward you. "

But the lad was not a fool; he went into the garden and cut a cabbage, and after he had tied it up in a handkerchief, took it to his aunt. " Have you brought me the shoes, Ivanouchka? " — " Yes. " — " Give them to me, that I may try them on! " — " First, earn them. " He led her into a barn, placed the handkerchief under her head, and began to futter her. During the operation, the cabbage which served as a pillow, gave forth a series of squeaks. " You may cry or not, " she said, " but you shall soon be on my feet. " — " You may also eat them boiled, " remarked the nephew.

LXXI

Curious names.

A peasant lived with his wife. He went one day to plough in his field, and hardly had he drawn a furrow than he turned up a casket full of money. The *moujik* was delighted; he picked up the casket but just as he did so there appeared a soldier who had seen the money, and said: " Look here, peasant! That money is mine. If you restore it to me, you shall find a casket full of money in every furrow you make. "

The peasant thought it over, and finished by giving up his find to the soldier. Then he set to work again; drew a furrow, and found nothing; drew a second and was not more fortunate. " Evidently I don't plough deep enough, " he thought, and drove the share in deeper. The horse could hardly pull the plough, and still there was no treasure. The *moujik's* wife came to bring him his dinner and reproached him bitterly. " What a hard task-master you are! You have not the fear of God before your eyes ; look how you have made the poor horse sweat! Why do you plough so deep? " — " Listen, wife, " replied the peasant; " as soon as I came into the field and had drawn my first furrow, I unearthed a casket full of money, but the devil then brought here a soldier. " If you give me that money! " he said, " you shall find as many similar caskets as you make furrows today! " I gave him the casket, and set to work, but as I unearthed nothing, I said to myself. 'No doubt I don't drive the share deep enough!' and I made the furrows deeper. I have worked all the day and have found nothing. " — " What a fool you are! Fortune came in your way and you did not know how to keep it. But which way did the soldier go? " —" He went in that direction. " —" Well, I will catch him yet! "

And the peasant woman and her boy set off in pursuit of the soldier.

After she had walked some distance, she saw in front of her, on the road, a soldier who carried a casket in his hands. She overtook him. " Good day, soldier! Where are you going? " —" I am on furlough, my dear. " — " And for what village are you bound? " —" To such a place. " — " Well, I also am going there; let us make the journey together. " — " Be it so. " The woman and the soldier journeyed on together, and talked as they went. " What is your name, my dear? " —" Ah, soldier, my son and I have names which must not be spoken " " Why not? There may be a shame in stealing, perhaps; but there can be no shame in telling a name. " —" Well, you see; I am called Naserou(1) and my son Nasral(2) " — " Bah! what does that matter? "

They arrived at an inn where they determined to pass the night; as soon as the soldier was asleep, the peasant woman took away the casket, woke her son, and the two returned home. When he woke the soldier looked all around him, and not finding the money, began to call, " Naserou, Naserou! " The master of the house heard him. " Go and do that in the privy, soldier, " he said. When the soldier found that the woman did not reply to his

(1) I must shit.
(2) I have shit.

cries, he began to call the boy; " Nasral, Nasral!! "
Thereupon the inn-keeper flew into a rage.
" Cursed trooper! He has made a mess in the
room. " He took the soldier by the shoulders,
and turned him out of doors.

LXXII

The *pope* and the *Tsigane*.

In a certain country there lived a *Tsigane*,
whose father was very old. The old man fell se-
riously ill, and took to his bed. His son cared
for him at first, but afterward ceased to pay any
attention to him. If his father asked for drink or
anything else, the *Tsigane* pretended not to hear
him, and had but one desire — that his father
might die as quickly as possible. " Oh, my son,
my son, " said the old man, " You do not seem to
look upon me as your father, and yet it was I
who begot you. " — " That be damned for a
tale, " replied the son. " It was not for my sake
that you begot me, but for your own pleasure.
Return to your mother's belly, or I will cut you
in two. " The old man sighed and was silent.

A short time after that he died. The body was
dressed and laid out on a bench, some incense
was burned in the *izba*, and all the usual preparations made, and then the *Tsigane* went to fetch

a *pope*. " Good day, *batouchka*! " " Good day,
Tsigane; what news? "   —" My father is dead;
come and bury him. "   —" Is it possible that he
is dead. " " He is dead, and died peacefully. As
he lies upon the bench he looks like a Christ,
with his beard so nicely combed. Come to our
house, pray, and see how white his body is. I
believe, *batouchka*, that he was a saint, and
exhales an odor of incense! "   —" Well, *Tsigane*,
have you any money to pay for the funeral? " —
" Why should I give you any money? For that old
carcass laid out on the bench, who is as black as
charcoal, and shows his teeth like a mad dog? Is
it for that you expect money? Very well! Don't
come and bury him! I will drag him here by the
feet, and you may do what you like with him! "
— " Very good, very good, " replied the *pope*,
" I will come at once and bury him. "

The *Tsigane* returned home and the priest
came shortly afterwards. A funeral service was
performed, the body was put in a coffin, taken to
the cemetery and buried. " Cannot you give me
a fee of some sort for having buried your father? "
said the *pope* to the *Tsigane*, " It will be a sin
on your part if you do not. " " Ah, *batouchka*, " replied the son of the dead man, " you know
yourself that the *Tsiganes* never have any money.
I had a few groschens but I expended them all on
the Requiem; but have patience, *batouchka*, and
wait till the fair takes place. I shall get some

money then, and, I will pay you. " — " Very good, my son; I will wait. "

The fair took place and the *Tsigane* went to the town and sold his horses. The priest also had business at the fair, and the two men met. " Look here, *Tsigane,* " began the *pope*; " It is time that you paid me. " —" Time that I paid you? But do I owe you any money, then? " — " Of course you owe me something. I buried your father. " — " Ah! that is what bothered me. I have been looking everywhere for my father, and could not find him. Other men have fathers to sell their horses for them, and I haven't. So it was you, old goat-beard who buried my father! " He seized the *pope* by the beard, knocked him down, and drawing the whip from his girdle began to flog him. " Then it is your fault, old goat-beard, that my father is not now alive. I will give you a good thrashing with my knout. " The *pope* had great difficulty in escaping from the hands of the *Tsigane*; he hurried away as quickly as possible, and from that day ceased to demand any money from such a debtor.

LXXIII

The good *pope*.

A *pope* hired a man-servant, took him home, and said to him: " Now, my man, do your work well, and I will never desert you. " — The servant had been in his place a week when mowing began. " Now, my friend, " said the *pope*, " with God's permission we will pass a pleasant evening, and tomorrow morning we will go and cut the hay. " — " Very good, *batouchka*. "

The next morning they rose early. The *pope* said to his wife: " Give us some breakfast, *matouchka*, we are going into the field to cut the hay. " The *pope's* wife laid the table. The priest and his servant sat down and breakfasted copiously: Then the farmer said: " We will take the opportunity to dine now, and then we can mow without interruption till mid-day. " — " As you please, *batouchka; * be it so; let us dine. " —" Serve the dinner, *matouchka*, " the *pope* said to his wife. She obeyed and they again began to eat. " Since we are at table, " said the *pope* then to the servant, " if you like, my friend, we will now have our snack, and then we will mow till supper-time. " — "As you wish, *batouchka;* so be it, let us have our snack! " — The *pope's* wife served the snack, of which the men partook largely. " Suppose we were to sup at the same time? " then remarked the priest. " We will pass the night in the field, and tomorrow we can set to work the first thing. " — " Willingly, *batouchka*. " — The pope's wife served the supper. After this repast the men rose from table. The servant took off his smock.

and prepared to retire. " Where are you going, friend? " asked the *pope*. — " Where am I going? You know yourself, *batouchka*, that after supper the next thing to do is to go to bed. " He went off to the barn, and slept till the following morning. From that day henceforth the *pope* took care never to give his servant breakfast, dinner, snack, and supper, all at once.

LXXIV

A wager.

A *pope* kept an inn on the high road, and many *moujiks* who were returning home after having earned some money by working abroad, used to lodge or dine in this house. One day the *pope* said to a young man: " Well, friend; have you had plenty of work, and made plenty of money? " — " I am taking home five-hundred rubles. " — " That is good business. Will you wager with me those five-hundred rubles against a thousand that I will give you if you win? " — " What sort of bet would you have? " — " This is it: Spend twenty-four hours in my house; drink and eat as much as you please, but you must not relieve yourself. If you fulfil this condition you win your wager. On the other hand, if you do not, I win. " — " So be it, *ba-*

touchka. " The bet was accepted. The *pope* then put on the table all sorts of victuals and drink. The young man ate and drank till he could no longer breathe. The pope shut him up in a private room.

Before the day finished, the peasant felt the need of relieving himself, and could hold out no longer. What was to be done? " Open the door, *batouchka,* " he cried at last. " I have lost my bet. " The *pope* took all the young man's money, and sent him home completely cleaned out. This method of increasing his income greatly pleased the priest, and he cleaned out several other *moujiks* by means of the same trick. The news of this spread throughout the neighboring villages and hamlets, and a cunning peasant who had returned home with less than a groschen in his purse, resolved to pay the *pope* back in his own coin. He went to the inn, and said he wished to pass the night there. " Where do you come from? " —" I have been working away from home, and now I am returning. " " Are you bringing back plenty of money? '' " About fifteen-hundred rubles. " On hearing this, the *pope* almost jumped for joy. " Look here, " he said, " We will make a bet. Eat and drink to your heart's content, but for twenty-four hours you are not to relieve yourself in any way. If you fulfil this condition, I will pay you fifteen-hundred rubles; if you fail you must pay me. Is that agreed? " — " So be it, *batouchka.* " The peasant sat down to table and began to regale himself; the *pope* no sooner set food and drink before him than they were devoured. After he had gorged himself, the peasant rolled on the ground and went to sleep, and the pope locked him in the room.

In the night the *moujik* awoke with a violent desire to s..t. He tried to break open the door, but it resisted all his efforts. But the *moujik* saw the *pope's* huge cap, hung on a nail, so he took it, more than half filled it, then put it back in its place, and went to sleep again.

The twenty-four hours being up, the man knocked at the door. " Open, *batouchka* ! " The *pope* opened the door, looked around, and could not see any excrement anywhere. Then the peasant pressed him to pay. The priest made a wry face, but he was obliged to pay the fifteen-hundred rubles. " What is your name, cursed scoundrel? " he asked, " I will not let you leave the house till I know. " — " I am called, Kakofi, *batouchka* ! " replied the *moujik*. He took his money and departed. When he was alone, the *pope* thought the matter over, and deeply regretted his fifteen-hundred rubles. The idea came to him that he would take a ride to get rid of his grief. He took down his hat which was hung on the wall, but when he put it on, the disgusting contents of the *chapka* flowed down over his head, neck, and shoulders. This increased his anger, and he hastily rushed out of the house into the courtyard,

and mounted his horse. On the high road he met
a lot of wagoners. " My children, have you seen
Kakofi (1) ? " asked the *pope*. " How you are, *batouchka*? You look handsome and no mistake
about it. Who made you in that mess? " —Thereupon the *pope* returned to his house.

LXXV

How I am.

In a certain country there lived a peasant who
was a great rogue. Having stolen a hundred
rubles he fled from his village, and after he had
walked a long distance, he presented himself at
the house of a *pope*, from whom he demanded
hospitality for the night. " Enter; there is room
here for you, " replied the *pope*. The peasant
entered, undressed himself, and lay down on a
bench. It occurred to him that he would like to
see how much money he had about him, so he
pulled it out of his pocket, and began to count
it. The *pope* saw how the peasant was occupied
(they are quick at noting things of that sort) and
said to himself. " Why look! He is dressed in

(1) There is a pun here in the Russian original.
Kakofia means " how I am, " and it is in this sense that
the wagoners take the question.
(2) See the previous story.

rags, and yet what a lot of money he has. I will give him drink, and when he is drunk I will rob him. "

A short time afterwards the *pope* approached the *moujik* and said: " Come, let us sup together, " replied the other. They sat down to supper, and the *pope* filled his guest's glass with brandy as often as it was empty, and gave him no rest. These repeated libations made the peasant drunk, and he rolled helplessly on the floor; then the priest took his money, locked it up in a cupboard and laid the *moujik* on a bench.

The next morning when the visitor awoke, he found his pockets had been cleared, and guessed what had occurred, but what was he to do? If he complained to the police, it would certainly be asked where he had obtained the money, and how it came to be in his possession, and he would only get himself into trouble. The *moujik* therefore went away for one month, two months, three months. He roamed about in different places, and at last he said to himself: " It is certain that the *pope* must now have forgotten me. I will disguise myself so that he shall not recognise me, and go to his house, and make him pay for the trick he played me the other day. "

He went to the priest's house; the *pope* was not at home and his wife was alone in the house.

" Allow me to pass the day here, *matouchka!* "
—" Be it so, enter. " The peasant entered, and
sat on a bench. " What is your name, friend?
From whence come you? " — " I am called
Kakofi, *matouchka*, and I come from afar; I am
on pilgrimage. " There was a book on the
pope's table: The *moujik* took it, turned over
the leaves, muttered between his teeth as though
he were reading, and then burst into tears.
" Why do you weep, friend? " demanded the
pope's wife — " Why should I not weep? It
says in the Holy Scriptures that every one shall
be punished according to his sins, and I am a
great sinner. I have committed so many bad
actions that I do not know, *matouchka*, how
God can overlook my faults. " — "Do you
know how to read and write, friend? " —" Oh,
yes, *matouchka*. I cannot complain in that respect, thank goodness. " " And do you know the
church service? " —" Do I know it? I should
think so, *matouchka*. I learnt it in my infancy.
I know all the services of the church. " —" Well,
friend, we have no sacristan; ours has gone to
bury his brother. Can you, tomorrow, help my
husband to celebrate the mass? " —" Certainly,
matouchka; why not? "

The *pope* arrived, and his wife related all to
him. He was delighted, and set before the *moujik* the best he had in the house. The next morning the two men went together to the church.

The *pope* began to say the mass; the peasant stood in the choir, and remained mute as a fish. " Why, instead of singing, do you stand there, and say nothing? " cried the priest. " Be it so; I will sit down, since you object to my standing up, " replied the peasant, and he sat down. " Why do you sit there and not sing ? " — " Very well; I will lie down! " And he lay on the floor. The *pope* took him by the shoulders and turned him out of the church, but he himself remained to finish the service.

The peasant returned to the priest's house. " Well; is divine service finished? " asked the *pope's* wife. —" Yes, *matouchka*. " —" But where is my husband? " —" He has stayed at the church to perform a funeral. But he sent me to ask for his new cloak lined with cloth, and his beaver hat; as he has a long journey to make, he wants to be warmly clad. " Whilst the *pope's* wife went to seek the articles required, the *moujik* went behind the *izba*, took off his bonnet, made filth in it, and placed it on a bench; then he took the *pope's* cloak and beaver hat, and decamped.

The priest, the mass being finished, returned to the house; his wife, seeing him clad in his old cloak, asked him what he had done with the new one. — " What do you mean by the new one? " — An explanation followed, and both saw that the peasant had deceived them. In his wrath, the *pope* seized the bonnet full of filth, which was lying on the bench, put it on his head, and ran through the village searching for the thief, but, on putting it on, the contents of the bonnet ran all over his face, and he was covered with filth. He entered hastily into an *izba*. " Have you seen Kakofi? " he asked the master of the house. " I see how you are, *batouchka*! you are clean! " All whom the *pope* questioned made the same reply. " What fools they are, " he said to himself, " they don't know what they are talking about. " He went through all the village, but could obtain no information about the thief. " Well! " he thought, "that which falls out of the cart is lost! "

He returned home, took off his cap, and when his wife set eyes upon him, she cried out: " Oh, *batouchka*; your face is all covered with pimples. " " What nonsense are you talking? " replied the *pope*. He passed his hand over his face and dirtied his fingers most abominably. So ends the story.

LXXVI

The merchant's wife and the clerk.

A merchant, — an old dotard, — had married a young wife, and he had several clerks.

His chief clerk was named Potap; he was a handsome youth, and made love to his master's wife, flirted with her, and succeeded in winning her love. It was noticed, and the merchant was informed of it. He said to his wife: " Look here, my dear; people say that you live with my clerk Potap — " — " Do you think I would do such a thing! Don't believe what people tell you; believe your own eyes! " —" They say that he has for a long time enjoyed your favors. Could we not prove him in some way? " — " Very well, " replied his wife " Listen to me. Dress yourself up in my clothes; go to him in the garden (you know

where he lodges) and say to him in a low voice!
I have left my husband to come to you! You
will then hear what he says. " — " So be it, "
replied the merchant.

The young woman, taking advantage of a
favorable opportunity, told the clerk what he
had to do. " When my husband comes, " she
said; " give him a sound thrashing that he will
remember for a long time. "

The merchant waited till night-fall, dressed
himself from head to feet in his wife's clothes,
and went into the garden of the clerk's house.
" Who is there? " asked the clerk. " It is I, my
love! " replied the merchant in a low voice. —
" What is the meaning of this visit? " — " I
have left my husband and come to you. " —
" Ah! You whore. It is said already that I make
love to you, and you want, it seems, to disgrace
me with my master! " So saying he loaded the
merchant with blows on his shoulders, back, and
sides, and, in short, gave him a thorough thrashing. " Don't come here again, you bitch, to dishonor me. Nothing in the world should induce
me to stoop to such infamies! "

The merchant escaped as best he could, returned in haste to his wife, and said: " No, my dear;
they may tell me as much as they like that you
live with the clerk, but I will not believe it. He
insulted, abused, and beat me, and I had a good
deal of trouble to get away from him. " — " You

see! And you believe whatever is told you! "
replied his wife; and from that day, she lived
with the clerk without any fear.

www.ingramcontent.com/pod-product-compliance
Lightning Source LLC
Chambersburg PA
CBHW010733270326
41935CB00015B/1795